A HISTORY OF
DEATH AND BURIAL
IN NORTHAMPTONSHIRE

A HISTORY OF
DEATH AND BURIAL
IN NORTHAMPTONSHIRE

PETER HILL

AMBERLEY

First published 2011

Amberley Publishing
The Hill, Stroud
Gloucestershire GL5 4EP

www.amberleybooks.com

British Library Cataloguing in Publication Data.
A catalogue record for this book is available from the British Library.

ISBN 978-1-4456-0462-6

Typesetting and Origination by Amberley Publishing.
Printed in Great Britain.

CONTENTS

Acknowledgements 7

Introduction 8

1. The Social Background 11
2. Pre-Christian Northamptonshire 20
3. Forms of Burial 28
4. The Art of Dying 77
5. Written in Stone 88
6. Images of Death 117
7. Working in Stone: The Masons and Their Materials 139
8. Tolling the Bells 144

Appendix 1. Brasses 146
Appendix 2. Hatchments 148
Appendix 3. Recumbent Stone Effigies 149
Appendix 4. Parish Registers 151
Appendix 5. Field Names 154
Appendix 6. 'The Forgotten Burial Place' 156

Bibliography 157

ACKNOWLEDGEMENTS

I would like to thank those individuals who have provided useful information or assisted me in looking at headstone inscriptions and unusual features around the county, among them Julie Banham, Ted Barlow, Maureen Basford, Andy Chapman, Tony Coales, Janet Collins, Margaret Craddock, Audrey Forgham, Joyce Griggs, Angela Jones, Steve Mitchell, Alma O'Neil, Tracey Partida, Mike Taylor, Alan Tebbutt, Philip Walker and Ros Willatts. My appreciation also extends to those descendants of certain families who helped with background material, in particular Tessa Le Sueur, Stephen Hall and Bill Richardson. The pioneering work of Katharine Esdaile and Frederick Burgess must also be mentioned, the latter's early survey of memorials in the Midlands having been an inspiration for all those with a sense of adventure, curiosity and inspiration. My thanks also go to Kettering Museum, Desborough Heritage Centre, the British Library, the National Archives and retired farmer David Palmer, whose land was available for a lengthy archaeological dig over a number of recent years, and who has recorded other notable excavations and events in his area. Past conversations with eminent archaeologists like Francis Pryor and Mike Parker Pearson have also proved enlightening, as has my own work on digs, especially those where burials from the Romano-British and Anglo-Saxon periods have materialised, and my involvement with *Time Team* visits to Nassington, Great Easton and Medbourne.

The parish registers now kept at the Northamptonshire Record Office have been crucial in matching up and deciphering headstone inscriptions, particularly where the latter have been hardly legible. Similarly, the hard work of those members of the Northamptonshire Family History Society involved in scouring churches and churchyards (including Nonconformist churches) and recording the results in the ongoing series of memorial inscription booklets has been invaluable.

INTRODUCTION

A study of death and burial practices through the ages can be a daunting task, especially with so much having disappeared, or in the process of disappearing. However, with perseverance and determination, it can also be one of the most rewarding assignments. By bringing all the various strands together, one can throw light on an important part of our ancestors' lives.

In common with any other county in Britain, Northamptonshire has a rich heritage of social history within the confines of its churches and churchyards. The theme can seem somewhat deceptive – and perhaps morbid – at first glance, but it contains and unravels an untold wealth of colourful, intriguing information – much of it not recorded elsewhere in documents and other sources.

Headstones, tombs, memorials, obituaries, and church furnishings are like a book, which, when 'opened', reveals an overflowing cornucopia of stories among the inscriptions, dates, names, occupations, symbols, secrets, superstitions, poems, images – and even puns. In fact, the subject is not so much about death, but rather life itself – its hopes, joys, fears and trials.

Tragically, such a great repository of social history has been allowed to decay over the years, as certain furnishings inside churches have been defaced or stolen. Outside, in the churchyard, much of the fabric has been subjected to erosion by the elements, lichen, moss and ivy, general neglect, or a combination of some of these, causing inscriptions to become illegible, part-illegible or non-existent. Other stones have been more fortunate, having fallen over with their inscriptions facing the ground, but, even so, little or no effort has been made to re-erect them, although the problem has partially been solved, albeit slowly, since the 1974 Health and Safety Act and the 1984 Occupiers Liability Act – which covers the potential danger of unsafe headstones, and ultimate family responsibility for maintenance. Several councils now have a Memorial Safety Inspection Policy, as a result of which churchyard monuments are tested manually and with a pressure gauge (monuments have to resist up to 35 kg of force). Unstable monuments are then bound and staked at the rear, with some councils, particularly in Scotland, retrenching and re-erecting fallen stones. Families are contacted beforehand about the procedure and are ultimately responsible for costs.

A modern trend has been to level churchyards for convenience and management, for example that at Wellingborough, where at least the headstones have been re-sited against the churchyard walls, and at Desborough, where a number have been repositioned by railings adjoining a footpath. In other cases, like Corby, the churchyards have been truncated for road building, or even building development, necessitating reburial or the removal of monuments. At Towcester, where the original churchyard was closed in 1885, a great many headstones have been laid flat so that it is impossible to read the inscriptions – a tragic situation because of the unique features of some of the monuments.

Quite often a look through parish registers and independent record books can help match names and dates, but in other cases it is too late, for although the entries for burial are recorded, a virtually erased stone makes it impossible to make any connection.

However, the situation has improved in some respects. There is now a headstone-cleaning company based in Kettering that offers a professional, safe and sympathetic service that goes some way towards restoring some inscriptions. There is also an exciting development in the world of technology, where new scanning techniques developed by US scientists at Carnegie Melton University help detect faint curvatures and linear features on stone surfaces, and try to fit the shapes to templates of letters, phrases and patterns derived from archaeological research into churchyard epitaphs. Any new patterns are added to its template database, widening the scope for success – the more the system is developed and used, the faster and better it will become in determining what is missing or has been lost.

One remarkable pioneering effort took place in the summer of 1959, when the pupils of Corby Grammar School took on the task of recording all 235 of the parish churchyard headstones and monuments, and the type of stone used. The churchyard was officially closed in 1899, replaced by a new site at the northern end of the village. To supplement the findings, photographs were taken – in retrospect a good move, as more than the fifty-four noted at the time have since become illegible, and part of the churchyard was removed in 1970. When the school had completed its survey, it was hoped that other schools would take on a similar assignment on behalf of their communities but sadly little, if anything, of a similar nature has materialised.

Later, however, in 1997 and the following year, a group of adult members of the WEA at Helmdon decided to document the inscriptions in the village churchyard. At the same time, the Northamptonshire Family History Society began the Herculean task of recording the county's many inscriptions, and at the time of writing, groups of volunteers have been to over 140 places (parish churches and Nonconformist burial grounds) – about 50 per cent coverage – and have published their results in a series entitled Memorial Inscription Booklets, which includes the inscriptions on each stone as well as a plan of each churchyard. It is a demanding task, requiring time, patience and lots of dedication. Attention will now be focused on the little-documented south-west area of Northamptonshire around Brackley, Daventry and Towcester.

Researching, lecturing and running courses here and abroad over the years has been very profitable in forming the matrix for this book, as it has with my previous efforts. Another great advantage has been involvement with two groundbreaking projects focusing on social history, landscape interpretation, buildings and churches, namely 'People of the Forest', which covered much of the north of the county, and 'Rose of the Shires', which has covered large swathes in the central and southern areas, plus the old Soke of Peterborough. Producing 'statements of significance' for the PCCs and the diocese and, in some cases, helping them put together church guides has also been particularly satisfying. The amount of interest shown by the many people who came to our sessions rewarded our efforts more than expected, and in some cases their local knowledge helped to make our task a little easier, by going some way towards solving the occasional problems that cropped up. Taking numerous groups around churchyards also gave us the opportunity to dispel one or two myths and misconceptions about such places.

A thorough and comprehensive study of death and burial requires delving into several subject areas, ranging through religion, customs, folklore, superstition, fashion, heraldry, archaeology, demography, health and medicine to more exotic-sounding specialist subjects like thanatology, palaeography, epigraphy, codicology and semiotics. It also requires a grasp of Latin, medieval French and, to a lesser degree, Middle English. Countless documents and records have been trawled through, including parish registers, churchwardens' accounts, wills, bequests, Nonconformist records, school logbooks, diaries, letters, obituaries, family papers, personal memoirs and newspaper files. The results have been extremely gratifying – and eye-opening.

Also enlightening have been the seminars I have run at the universities of Nottingham and Dundee, in which attendees and colleagues have been most forthcoming with information about burials and inscriptions within their locality – which in turn have led to new areas for further investigation, exploration and comparison.

Everything has been covered to give as wide and accurate a picture as is possible. I hope you find the end product worthwhile, edifying, and, perhaps most of all, encouraging enough for you to go out and explore some of the places and subject matter for yourself, and to discover the rich heritage the county still has to offer – before much of it disappears.

Finally, despite the nature of the subject, there is always a place for humour. One of the county's renowned poets and dramatists, John Dryden, wrote the following epigram on his wife's demise:

> Here lies my wife: here let her lie!
> Now she's at rest, and so am I.

Dr Peter Hill
2011

1

THE SOCIAL BACKGROUND

Before looking at death and burial, it is necessary to look at the general historical background of Northamptonshire and examine the social, economic and demographic changes that have affected people's beliefs, customs and ways of life up to the present day.

Until the Industrial Revolution in the second half of the eighteenth century, daily life was much less complicated than our modern *progressive* life, which is geared to improvement, development and change. For our ancestors, life was short, harsh, violent, painful, and geared to the seasons, i.e. it was *cyclical*. Theirs was a fatalistic, 'make the most of it' existence in the face of poor harvests, famine, epidemics, warfare, sickness and poverty. They remained in the same locality for most of, if not all, their lives. Travel was non-existent for the majority, except in times of warfare. For most folk, walking would be the normal means of getting about – mainly to the next village.

Their behaviour was entirely different to ours. Often they would take justice into their own hands. In church there would be spitting, swearing, cussing, fighting, joking, gossiping, urinating, dogs running around, babies crying, and later, when seating and sermons in English were introduced in the Tudor period, jostling for pews, shouting, and mocking the priest or other members of the congregation.

If anyone upset the harmony of the community, a common form of social disapproval would be shown in the form of 'lowbelling', also known around the county variously as 'drumming out', 'banging out', 'panning out', 'rough music', 'riding the stang' or the 'Skimmington ride'. The offenders might be malicious gossipers and scandalmongers, wife-beaters, adulterers, or anyone committing incest. Apart from making as much noise as possible outside the dwelling of the offender(s) for a prolonged period, there would often be an effigy of the culprit, or someone dressed like him or her, carried in a seat on the shoulders of various pall bearers, and set alight (like the image of Guy Fawkes) at their destination. In most cases the message was put across strongly enough to result in the offender moving away to another village or town. Lowbelling continued to take place in Northamptonshire until 1936 (and is still performed annually, albeit as a 'fun-only' event at Broughton, where the 'Tin Can Band' create pandemonium from midnight during the second week of December).

Weddings, of course, were one of the highlights of people's lives, but they were not the most important. A non-religious 'contract' was commonly held to be especially meaningful – and necessary – as a preliminary before the church ceremony. Known as 'hand fasting', it was a two-fold process performed in front of a group of witnesses including members of the two families involved, beginning with the future husband kissing his bride-to-be, and then the presentation of some form of gift, which might be a ring or something of particular value. In many ways, this was like an engagement, but it was also a way of sanctioning sexual relations between the couple before the church wedding. In fact, many a bride was pregnant at the altar, some heavily so.

The actual church wedding itself would take place a minimum of three weeks after the issuing of the banns, which were published for anyone wishing to object to the union. Mondays and Thursdays were formerly considered to be the best days for a wedding, but this was not a hard and fast rule. Often the bridal pair were fumigated with brambles as a preamble, and the smoke was thought to drive away any harmful influences that might spoil the union. The bridal veil had a similar purpose. The first stage of the wedding would take place in the porch, where the couple were blessed. Then they would proceed to the altar for the service itself, after which, on leaving the church, they would carry flowers, or be accompanied by a small child, and then meet with a hail of corn from onlookers, the grain being a fertility symbol (like the flowers and child), a means of encouraging a fruitful union.

Sometimes a form of secular marriage ceremony was carried out, like the hand fasting, but in this case *after* the church wedding. A circlet of flowers or evergreens would be placed on the heads of the couple, who would then stand with their backs against a tree (another fertility symbol) while a crowd of villagers formed a wide circle, dancing around them three times (a potent number) and singing a particularly bawdy song with suggestive lyrics.

Religion played a dominant role in the lives of many, with church attendance compulsory for several centuries. For those who could afford the time and money, making a pilgrimage played a vital part in their lives. A blessing, vow, and protection against danger were deemed a necessary prerequisite before embarking on such a journey, either in the form of an amulet, or by engraving a small votive cross, usually with pits or small lines at the end of each arm, on a pillar or exterior wall of a church. Sometimes this was done after the pilgrimage as a sign of thanksgiving for a safe journey.

Remains of saints and reliquaries were of special importance during the medieval era. In the church at Brixworth, which was also the site of a monastery founded by Sexwulf, Bishop of Mercia, at some time before 675, there is definite evidence of a reliquary – possibly two, at various stages in time. Reliquaries were good money-spinners, attracting pilgrims from far and wide, the most popular items being a bone or piece of clothing (like pieces of the cross, or phials of Christ's blood), the nail clippings of St Edmund, the girdle of the Virgin Mary, the penknife of St Thomas à Becket, and the many heads of John the Baptist; all were duplicated or manufactured en masse. Despite the deception, these were believed to work wonders on disease, ailments and infirmities and to give spiritual inspiration and good fortune. (The Reformation finally put paid to such a fraudulent practice.) The church had a barrel-vaulted ambulatory or 'ring crypt' that could be entered by pilgrims and penitents from the chancel, the passageway providing access to shrines where relics of saints could be viewed or, in some cases, touched. If there was a reliquary, it has long since disappeared from the now-roofless vestiges of the ambulatory. However, in 1809, workmen engaged in altering the pews uncovered a small human throat bone and a piece of parchment (one theory gives a possible connection with the European missionary St Boniface). These were later transferred to the hands of a parishioner for safekeeping before being returned to the church in 1875, and are currently in the Lady Chapel.

Until the fourteenth century, Northamptonshire, like the rest of the country, had seen a growth in population and an increasingly strong economy. Much of the countryside became open plough land, which provided plentiful grain for everyone. (Until the eighteenth century, most of the population was engaged in some form of agricultural occupation and had a simple lifestyle, with basic foodstuffs and dwellings.) Then disaster struck.

Between 1315 and 1321, a series of devastating crop failures hit everyone, rich and poor. It was the result of extremely cold, wet summers and early frosts and snowfall, which gave the grain little chance to germinate. Instead it rotted, leading to food shortages, widespread famine – and scores of thefts. Cattle and sheep were depleted by murrain, and those beasts that survived had great difficulty ploughing the soggy terrain. On top of all this, a typhoid-like epidemic hit the human population in 1316. But this was nothing compared to what happened next.

First came a great pestilence, the so-called Black Death (a name invented in the nineteenth century) in 1348–49. It wiped out between a third and half of the population, and was followed by a spate of lesser, although still lethal, epidemics of plague in 1361 and 1368–69, so much so that by the end of that century, the population was almost back to what it was at the time of the *Domesday Book*, almost two million. This began a transformation of the way society operated. The labour shortage led to demands for higher wages, and rents were reduced to take up vacated land. Many peasants/villeins became copyholders, an improvement on their previous servile status, which enabled them to pay the lord of the manor a rent for their land, with conditions, instead of performing all the customary services. Then land owners found an ideal solution in the form of sheep farming. Sheep did not need paying, and English wool was in great demand for its quality in Europe. Thus began the process of enclosing the land and its conversion to pasture, at the expense of the peasants. (This would accelerate in the sixteenth century, leading to a considerable number of DMVs – 'deserted medieval villages' – around the county.) The traumatic events also helped fuel the obsession with the afterlife, with the wealthier element of society founding endowment charities to sing masses for the dead in purgatory – some were founded by individuals, others by guilds. It would help relieve the fear of death and gain salvation through good deeds such as beautifying the church.

At the same time, the parish replaced the manor as the pivot of communal life between *c.* 1350 and 1520. Various 'ales' (community celebrations) were held – money-raising activities for the church and those in need (including newlyweds, and newborn babies). Parishes would begin to proudly assert their achievements and identity by 'name-calling' rival neighbouring villages in the form of 'folk rhymes' – a kind of 'we are better than you' situation that can still be seen today.

Then came the Reformation, which, apart from causing religious upheaval, took away the care of the sick, the elderly and the poor in almshouses ('hospitals') traditionally provided by the religious institutions that had now been dissolved. To counter the amount of misery and the number of vagrants that this had caused, a series of 'poor laws' were introduced, particularly in 1601, putting the burden on parishes, each of which appointed an overseer to collect a 'poor rate' from the community, thus forcing all able-bodied individuals to work. Unfortunately a number of the poor and destitute, both male and female, became vagrants, and they would wander into other villages, which could hardly cope with the burden of their own poor. The churchwardens or overseers would tie the intruders to the whipping post, give them a sound lashing, and send them back 'whence they came'. The situation was only partially eased with the passing of the 1723 Workhouse Test Act, ordering all villages and towns to provide a poorhouse for the needy within the community.

SUPERSTITION

Superstition played a paramount part in every facet of life. There were both favourable and unfavourable times for carrying out certain tasks or actions.

There were many superstitions regarding death, with such events usually heralded by an out-of-the-ordinary experience or sudden occurrence, such as a knock on the door for no apparent reason, a door opening by itself, a bodiless voice calling out a person's name, snowdrops taken into a house before Candlemas (1 February), flowering hawthorn taken into a house at any time, an owl hooting, a dog howling outside a window, or a bird flying down a chimney or into a house.

It was also important to ensure that the home was protected against any form of evil in the vicinity (whether human, demonic or natural, such as lightning or fire). Inverted images or inscriptions – being the reversal of normality – were believed to be especially efficacious, such as the raised letters 'Jehovah' and the date '1593' on a ceiling beam at Manor Farm, Wadenhoe. For the same purpose, religious verse was painted or placed near openings, such as those on the beams over fireplaces in houses at Hall Place in Brigstock, and West Street in Kingscliffe. Other methods included planting evil-repelling rowan and elder, plus thorny plants like holly and brambles, outside the home – these would have the additional benefit of being a deterrent to thieves, as would St John's Wort, or herb benet (wood avens) inside the house. Also fairly common was the placing of a live animal in the loft, where it would eventually die and remain earthbound, its spirit acting as a guardian of the home. There are two surviving examples of this practice – in this case mummified cats – on display in the museums at Kettering and Oundle. Today, thatchers still make effigies of animals and birds on cottage roofs, purely for decorative purposes.

During most of the seventeenth century there was a vogue for Bellarmine jars (or witch bottles) – stoneware vessels with bearded faces, filled with urine, hair, iron nails, etc. They were placed under the floor or over the threshold to prevent uninvited visitors such as witches from entering, the contents supposedly being anathema to such people.

PROTECTION

Evil was an ever-threatening presence in life. It was long thought that whenever anyone died, the Devil was waiting to seize control of the newly departed soul. It was also widely believed that all forms of evil hated the sound of bells, so a small 'passing bell' was kept in some homes and rung in order to drive malicious forces away.

Other measures were taken to protect the church itself. Many pathways leading through the churchyard to the church entrance were laid out diagonally, for, according to traditional belief, the Devil preferred straight lines; and if the church was fortunate enough to have been built on a circular site – which was usually indicative of a pre-Christian sacred area (such as those at Winwick and Finedon) – so much the better, for he would have 'nowhere to hide'. A circle was also considered to be a powerful shape, being a symbol of eternity, perfection and wholeness – the opposite of what the Devil represented and wanted. The north side of the church was the Devil's favoured location, the 'dark side' avoided by the sun (symbolising light and life), and the north door of the church was kept open during baptism, so that any evil lingering by the font could escape after the baby had undergone its spiritual cleansing and preparation for the life ahead. The font itself often had a hinged metal clasp (a hesp) fitted over an attached staple and locked to secure the lid so that holy water could not be taken out and used for evil purposes. Ten such 'staple fonts' survive in the county, from Duddington in the north to Roade in the south.

Apotropaic (protective) images were placed where the church was vulnerable, i.e. the 'weaker' parts of the church fabric – openings such as the belfry, windows, entrances and ceilings, where evil could attain easier access. They could be in the form of 'grotesques' – tongue pokers, face pullers (gurners), male and female exhibitionists (such as those at Cotterstock, Rothwell, Twywell and Isham), buttock bearers (as at Fotheringhay and Easton on the Hill), contorted faces, bestial scowling images and the Green Man. Serving a dual purpose – practical and spiritual – they could sometimes be admonitory, warning the congregation not to stray from 'the path of righteousness'. An example is the cat crouching over the mouse at the top of a buttress on the church of St Michael at Wadenhoe (this equates with the Devil pouncing on the unwary soul/sinner). Plants like vervain ('herb of the Cross') were placed in the porch, while in the churchyard, betony or sprigs of rowan would be effective in preventing any supernatural activity, especially on or near graves.

A piece of wasteland known as a 'jack' was sometimes put aside for the use of the Devil, to distract him from harming the crops growing on cultivated land in the parish. In Great Oakley this was known as 'Jack Arthur'. Similar measures were taken at certain village feasts, one notable example being the Crow Feast held at Wootton on St George's Day (originally 4 May), when a dead crow was put on display outside hostelries to ward off any evil influences that might spoil the occasion.

The figure of St Christopher was often painted on the wall of the north aisle of the church, opposite the normal entrance, and anyone seeing him was said to be safe from any harm that day. There are vestiges of his image at Slapton, Raunds, Glapthorn and Hargrave. An individual could also gain some degree of protection by wearing certain amulets around the neck, the most obvious being the crucifix (which also affirms one's faith) or an 'agnus dei', which was a piece of paper or a metal disc inscribed with a cross, or with a portion of written verse from the gospels. A gold coin, the angel, was introduced in 1485; such a powerful image would have been worn by the wealthier elements of society to protect against scrofula. A ring discovered in the 1890s on the site of Pipewell Abbey was engraved in Hebrew, its wording used as a charm against epilepsy and toothache. Other popular 'charms' that might be worn or carried by a person were 'holy plants' like agrimony. Another plant, mugwort, was believed to give unlimited protection against mishaps, even death. In fact, there was a popular rhyme in the medieval period: 'If they'd drunk nettles in March, and mugwort in May,/So many fine maidens would not go to clay.' It was indeed a medicinal plant, and was also used for flavouring ale, as was ground ivy before the introduction of hops into England *c.* 1420. Mugwort's many qualities were ascribed to John the Baptist, who wore a girdle of it to protect him from danger while in the wilderness.

Certain types of stone were believed to have some kind of beneficial influence. At Great Addington the mutilated fifteenth-century alabaster effigy of Sir Henry Vere was believed to have curative powers, and scrapings taken from it, known as 'Vere Powders', were administered to the villagers' children when they were ill. A similar custom around the country as a whole was to take chippings from stone circles and other prehistoric monuments as lucky amulets.

On St Mark's Eve (24 April), or, later in the year, on All Hallows' Eve, groups of girls in the county would take turns watching over the doorway of a church during the day until sunset, when one of them would lay a branch or flower in the porch. She would then return at midnight with a number of volunteers to remove it and place it at the churchyard gate to await the outcome. It was believed that a marriage procession would materialise shortly afterwards. As the bride passed by, hanging on to the arm of her groom, the girl would notice that she had the same face, while the number of wedding attendants represented the number of months that were to elapse before the ceremony. However, if she were not to be married, the vision would be that of a funeral procession, with a coffin draped in a white sheet, borne on by bearers with no shoulders.

'A NIGHT FOR LOST SOULS'

Inevitably, churches and churchyards, with their proximity to the dead, would have supernatural connotations in the minds of many people. It was widely believed that the dead would rise at midnight to dance around the graveyard, for example. Some villages had a tradition of hauntings by restless spirits who had died prematurely from illness, accident, suicide or murder, while others who had been so attached to a church in life left a psychic imprint, which would take bodily form when conditions allowed.

In his lengthy poem, 'A Parson's Night Visit to His Churchyard', Abner Browne, vicar of Pytchley (1832–51) and Gretton (1851–72), refers to a phenomenon sometimes known as 'grave lights', which at one time would have caused great consternation in the minds of anyone witnessing such a thing, but which were simply pieces of decayed coffin lids that had been brought to the surface, giving off a phosphorescent glow when mingling with the air.

> O'er yonder new-made grave, see, corpse lights gleam,
> With soft phosphoric haze of ghastly blue!
> Once awful portents would such glimmerings seem,
> Now known for coffin fragments thrown to view.

One of the most vivid apparitions supposedly once witnessed in the county was at Passenham, where a luminous skeletal figure with a broken neck was regularly seen riding through the churchyard, where it would eventually disappear among the headstones. Village tradition believed the figure to be that of a huntsman who had supposedly died in a riding accident long ago.

Today, the isolated and long-abandoned church of St John the Baptist stands in ruins at Boughton Green, about half a mile from the present village and its church. It formerly had a tradition of a spectral figure in wedding attire appearing after dark on Christmas Eve. During the early eighteenth century, when the church was still flourishing, a wedding took place with a tragic aftermath: shortly after the ceremony, the young husband of the eighteen-year-old bride suddenly died. The girl subsequently committed suicide. For many years it was considered unwise for anyone to walk alone by the churchyard during that evening, for she (or he) would greet the wayfarer, and, after enticing him or her into an embrace, a reunion was promised at the same place within a month – a fatal encounter, for that person would consequently die before the assignation.

Another unusual occurrence, albeit short-lived and relatively modern, took place in the daytime at Newton, near Geddington, where a smiling girl with long black hair and a white dress was said to have been seen on several occasions in the 1950s, hands clasped in prayer, passing out of the front wall of Manor Farmhouse and through the boundary wall opposite. Intriguingly, between 1971 and 1973, when the site behind the wall (a former churchyard) was excavated, an unusually large number of children were found to be among the graves.

In Great Oakley, a dwelling that has acted variously as the home of a vet and a vicar was at one time a place for 'laying out' the village dead, i.e. preparing the corpse in a winding sheet for burial. A former occupant, unaware of the one-time use of her home, was frequently disturbed by constant sobbing and animated conversation, the source of which she was unable to trace.

At the partly demolished church of Barnwell All Saints, there is a strangely shaped headstone, at present lying on its side against the chancel wall, where it had been taken from its former site near the entrance to the churchyard. For many years there was a strange tradition that it was that of a monk who formerly haunted the vicinity.

At Woodford, there have been cases in the past whereby volunteers doing flower arrangements or cleaning chores have been interrupted by an elderly, rosy-cheeked man in old-fashioned clothes suddenly appearing and calmly asking the way to a certain destination – then suddenly disappearing. Similarly, at Glapthorn, at least one volunteer has been disturbed by footsteps sounding audibly on the floor of the church, with no one in sight.

MORTALITY BILLS

> Learn then ye living! By the Months be taught
> Of all these Sepulchres, Instructors true,
> That soon or late, Death also is your Lot,
> And the next op'ning Grave, may yawn for you! (1788)

> Oh most delightful hour by Man
> Experienced here below.
> The hour that terminates his span,
> His folly, sin and woe! (1789)

From 1736 until 1871, it was customary in Northampton to issue an annual 'bill of mortality', listing the number of burials (and baptisms) that had taken place up to St Thomas's Day (21 December) that year. Initially covering only the parish of All Saints, it was soon extended to the whole town. A designated clerk would collect the data, which would be printed on broadsheets and issued to the mayor and prominent townspeople. From 1744, verses were added, together with depictions of skulls, bones and hourglasses. Various individuals were persuaded to contribute verses, the most renowned being William Cowper, who was staying at Weston Favell in 1787, and whose pieces (two portions of which open this section) appeared over the next seven years. A later contributor was John Askham, the Wellingborough shoemaker and poet whose verses appeared in 1868 and 1869. Two years later the custom was discontinued, at a time when people were living to a greater age than ever before.

MORTALITY IN THE NINETEENTH CENTURY

The average age of death until the end of the seventeenth century had been forty for a man, forty-five for a woman – and reaching that age could be a painful experience, with arthritis and teeth-related problems rife. The latter, together with stomach problems, were the most common forms of death (after 'old age'). Longevity would increase substantially during the next century, with certain improvements in hygiene and diet, but there were still major concerns. Epidemics, usually in the summer and of a water-borne nature, were frequent, such as cholera, dysentery, and typhoid (enteric fever). The causes were poor sanitation and drainage, especially the contamination of water by faeces. In winter, typhus was the biggest scourge. It was spread by lice and fleas as a result of overcrowded conditions, and little, if any, bathing; the worst outbreak occurred in 1837–38. Even influenza could prove to be a killer, with two

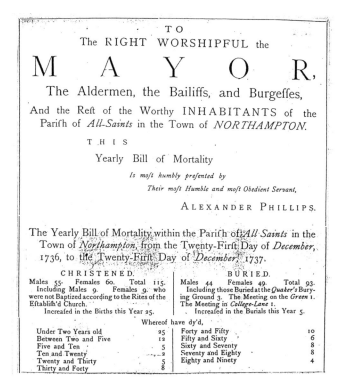

TO

The RIGHT WORSHIPFUL the

M A Y O R,

The Aldermen, the Bailiffs, and Burgeffes,

And the Reft of the Worthy INHABITANTS of the Parifh of *All-Saints* in the Town of *NORTHAMPTON.*

THIS

Yearly Bill of Mortality

Is moſt humbly prefented by

Their moſt Humble and moſt Obedient Servant,

ALEXANDER PHILLIPS.

The Yearly Bill of Mortality within the Parifh of *All Saints* in the Town of *Northampton,* from the Twenty-Firſt Day of *December,* 1736, to the Twenty-Firſt Day of *December,* 1737.

CHRISTENED.	BURIED.
Males 55. Females 60. Total 115. Including Males 9. Females 9. who were not Baptized according to the Rites of the Eſtabliſh'd Church. Increaſed in the Births this Year 25.	Males 44 Females 49. Total 93. Including those Buried at the *Quaker's* Burying Ground 3. The Meeting on the *Green* 1. The Meeting in *College-Lane* 1. Increaſed in the Burials this Year 5.

Whereof have dy'd,

Under Two Years old	25	Forty and Fifty	10
Between Two and Five	12	Fifty and Sixty	6
Five and Ten	5	Sixty and Seventy	8
Ten and Twenty	2	Seventy and Eighty	8
Twenty and Thirty	5	Eighty and Ninety	4
Thirty and Forty	8		

A typical eighteenth-century mortality bill for Northampton.

massive outbreaks in the 1830s, and more virulent strains evolving, the worst of which was the Spanish 'Flu of 1918. Childhood diseases such as scarlet fever, diphtheria and measles could also take their toll.

Smallpox was another virulent disease before vaccination was introduced by Edward Jenner in 1796. It was disfiguring and often fatal. Two particularly lethal epidemics hit the Northampton area, one in 1740, when 132 out of 899 people in the town who had contracted the disease are said to have died, and another in 1746–47. Nonconformist minister Philip Dodderidge described the epidemic hitting the area 'with very unusual violence in some neighbouring villages in which several of my Friends reside. I am told that in one of them between 40 and 50 Persons, most of them young, fell within very little more than a Week, and the Terror with which it fills these parts of the Country is exceeding great.' Even with vaccination, however, smallpox continued to be a scourge, particularly in 1839, when a quarter of deaths nationally were those of children under the age of one.

Consumption (tuberculosis) in pulmonary form was spread among family members via coughing and sneezing, as a result of infected milk and poor diet. It often led to tragic deaths among the young, as churchyard headstone inscriptions testify. Infant mortality was also high, as was that of young mothers, usually from puerperal (childbed) fever, an issue that was not seriously addressed until just before the turn of the next century. Also fairly common was 'overlaying' – the suffocation of an infant caused by carelessly turning it over by the mother or nurse.

2

PRE-CHRISTIAN
NORTHAMPTONSHIRE

Since the dawn of mankind, the prime concern of the human race has been survival, which demanded an ability to relate to the moods of the climate and the environment, and to come to terms with the many challenges they presented. One can imagine the alarm of primitive peoples on seeing an eclipse (thinking the sun was being devoured), or, more frequently, on hearing thunder (presumably caused by angry spirits). If a harvest failed, there would be misery, famine, sickness and death, and the people would look for the reason why such a thing had occurred. Therefore, a variety of means were put in place in an attempt to avoid recurrences of these and other misfortunes, many of them in the form of appeasement and obeisance to some supernatural source, for example a supernatural or ancestral deity in the Otherworld, Underworld, Heavens or earthly surroundings. Lives were harsh, precarious and short.

Allied to this was a wish for, or belief in, an afterlife. Life springs from a body, whether human, animal, plant, micro-organism or something celestial. But eventually all life must give way to death, and what happens after death has always intrigued mankind. We can either agree with the pragmatism of Shakespeare's Hamlet, who speaks of 'The undiscovered country from whose bourn/No traveller returns' or, like many cultures around the world, we can see death as a stage of life.

Prehistoric man would see rebirth in all forms of nature: the setting and the rising of the sun, the waning and waxing of the moon, day following night (light following darkness), the simple action of a snail disappearing into and re-emerging from its shell, a snake sloughing and renewing its skin, a male deer shedding and re-growing its antlers, the leaves of deciduous trees dying in the autumn only to reappear in the spring. Above all, as the year got older, people would experience the sun losing its heat and being at its weakest in the shortening, darker days of winter, only to slowly regain its strength in the spring and summer, accompanied by lighter and longer days.

Seeing all these manifestations of birth and rebirth in nature led to the idea that humans could and would either return here (perhaps in a different form) or experience a new life elsewhere. Later, with the introduction of Abrahamic religion, the new life would either involve a paradise or an inferno.

Since the sun was essential to life, early civilisations would construct their dwellings, fields, ritual sites and certain funerary monuments with the entrance facing the east or south-east, aligned with the rising sun, to receive the benefit of its life-giving rays. Even today, there are vestiges of this in the desire for south-facing gardens. Not dissimilar is *feng shui*, or living in harmony with one's surroundings, with its emphasis on locating the best position for a building and its rooms.

EARLY SETTLERS AND DISPOSAL OF THE DEAD

Hunter-gatherers constantly moved from place to place for their food. Around 4500 BC, the start of the Neolithic ('new stone') Age, they began to settle down in one place, practising animal husbandry and cultivating various crops. They also created causewayed enclosures – communal/tribal meeting places and market places, of which at least three are known to survive in the county, at Briar Hill (Northampton), Dallington and Southwick. However, we know little about how they disposed of most of their dead. The deceased were possibly thrown into rivers, except for those of a select few. Communal graves contained the dislocated bones of several individuals interred at different times, and are known generally as 'long barrows', although they could be trapezoid in form. The county has one known example, recently discovered near Stanwick as part of the Raunds Area Archaeological Project during the mid-1980s and early 1990s. Another, more unique kind, the 'oval' mound – which had a similar function and usage – seems to have been favoured in the Nene Valley area. They were in the form of a long rectangular mortuary enclosure with timber posts supporting a roof, which was subsequently sealed and covered with a mound of soil. The first was found beneath the surface prior to gravel extraction at Henslow Meadow in the parish of Aldwincle in 1968, and contained two inhumations, one with its bones disturbed, the other lying in a crouched position, i.e. sideways with knees drawn upwards. Hazelnut shells and pottery fragments (sherds) were also found in the soil.

A Bronze Age barrow in a field near Pipewell.

These Bronze Age collared urns were used for the cremated dead.

During the Bronze Age (*c.* 2200–1500 BC) emphasis was placed on *individual* burials (again of the more prestigious in the community) in *round* barrows, the body being interred in a pit and then covered over with a grassy mound. We have many more examples of these around the county, although many have been ploughed out over the years. Early burials were accompanied by a decorated drinking vessel and other items, such as a flint knife or a spearhead, for use in the afterlife. Such burials subsequently became known as 'beaker burials'. Interesting variations were discovered in round barrows at Henslow Meadow, where two adult men were found lying in wooden boat-shaped coffins, one accompanied by a boar's tusk and flint arrowheads. A sensational discovery was made later, again near Stanwick, in one of the round barrows being excavated. A huge limestone cairn was uncovered, topped with the remains of nearly 200 cattle (probably from a funeral feast). This would have covered a wooden structure, beneath which lay the body of a person of great importance, possibly a tribal chief. He

This Iron Age mirror found in Desborough was discovered in 1908. A replica is now in the town's heritage centre.

was found accompanied by an archer's wristguard and an assortment of other items, including conical jet buttons and an amber ring.

This custom gradually gave way to cremations placed in large cinerary containers (collared urns) until the dawn of the early Iron Age, *c.* 800 BC. Apart from one or two areas around the country, little is known about how Iron Age society in general disposed of their dead – we know more about how and where they lived. This is the converse of what we know about Bronze Age society. No organised burial sites can be found in Northamptonshire, but where remains are found, usually in isolation, they appear to have been treated in an impersonal manner, placed or cast into pits, or cremated, as in the previous era. However, there are exceptions, the main one being the fine example discovered at Desborough during ironstone quarrying in 1908, when a high-status lady's personal mirror (*c.* 50 BC–AD 23) was unearthed. With ornate fold-over symmetry, lyre pattern and a looped handle, it is an example of those produced in the West Country at the time, and like any similar reflective object, it would have had mystical significance, since it had the ability to give a view both forward and backward at the same time. It is now in the British Museum, but a fine copy can be seen at the

Desborough Heritage Centre. Other grave goods found with the mirror included a bronze ring, a thigh ornament, brooches and loom weights.

The later years of the era also saw an increased threat of warfare, leading to the construction of hillforts consisting of ramparts and ditches circling a hilltop to give a clear view of the surrounding countryside. One of several known sites in the county was at Rainsborough near Aynho, which suffered a particularly violent attack that resulted in its ramparts being pulled down, its massive gates set on fire, and at least one death, that of a young man found in the guard chamber with a hole in his skull from a blow. At Hunsbury Hill, the skeletons of a man and a horse, a bridle bit and part of a wheel from a chariot were discovered in the nineteenth century. Drilled skulls were also found. They were part of the war booty, and were seen as a powerful charm when placed outside dwellings and were attached to horses in battle as a protective device. Some are on display in Northampton Museum.

Burials became a more straightforward process with the coming of the Romans after AD 43; many of the occupiers' customs were adopted by local people. In line with superstitious practice, burials (with the exception of those of children) had to be made away from settlements, usually along roadsides, to avoid any problems with the disgruntled spirits of the dead. Parents usually got rid of any deformed or disabled offspring, because of their imperfections or potential inability to perform properly in society. Early burials were cremations in urns or wooden caskets, but from the late second century, inhumation gradually became fashionable. Inevitably, there were some strange deviations. In 1921, near Peterborough, bodies were found grouped in a circle with their heads facing the centre. At Barford – between Kettering and Corby – during road widening in 1964, a flat-topped conical mound was excavated. Beneath the mound was an eccentric 'stone circle' with two projecting arms. The primary burials had been robbed in previous centuries, but twenty-two 'secondary' burials of men, women and children were intact, the skeletons decapitated, and the skulls by their legs. This was common practice among the Romans, as were 'prone' (face down) burials, or bodies weighed down with stones – yet more ways of preventing the dead from causing unease among the living. Some wealthy Romanised Britons were buried in lead coffins and some families had private mausoleums. Sometimes an engraved grave marker was erected, such as that unearthed at Irchester in 1853, covering the burial of Amicius Saturninus, a Roman 'strator' (an official in charge of horses) whose inscription in Latin included a dedication to 'the departed spirits'.

When the Romans adopted Christianity in the fourth century, a change in burial practice took place. Formal 'flat' cemeteries appeared (as at Ashton, Laxton, Titchmarsh and Fotheringhay), with burials being made in regularly spaced trenches in neat rows, some bodies in shrouds, others in stone-lined cists or wooden coffins. They were buried with an east–west orientation (the head facing west) and there were no grave goods, since they would not need anything until the time of the Resurrection.

After the Roman withdrawal early in the fifth century, Angles, Saxons and Jutes integrated with the existing population. Unlike the locals, they were not yet Christianised and had their own forms of burial, similar to earlier civilisations, with both cremations and inhumations being customary. Respect for, or a continued use of, surviving burial

One of several late Romano-British inhumations excavated at a former Iron Age site at Wakerley during ironstone quarrying in 1973.

sites is evident in many places such as Easton Maudit, Piddington, Borough Hill and (more recently discovered) Rushton, where slabs of masonry from an adjoining bath house were used as grave cover for a burial surprisingly close (about 6 inches) to the surface. The slabs were no doubt employed to keep carnivorous animals away. Accompanying the remains in nearby graves were a round 'saucer' brooch favoured by Saxon women and a cruciform brooch favoured by Anglian women (who also dressed differently, using wrist clasps for their sleeves), all of which give a fascinating glimpse into the lives and cultures of two different Germanic peoples that had settled in the region.

People also had their own large, planned 'flat' cemeteries. Many of the earliest burials tended to be cremations, the remains of which were often placed in special handmade urns with a variety of stamped patterns (some of which were made with the carved underside of an antler) and distinctive protruding bosses, several of which were found in Barton Seagrave, Newton and Kettering, either during building development or ironstone quarrying between 1880 and 1929. Some are now on display in the town museum.

Thereafter it was a matter of choice, with inhumations being the favoured form and the bodies buried in a supine position (i.e. on their backs). At Nassington, during gravel extraction in 1942, fifty graves were unearthed, only three of which were cremations. There was a mixture of male and female, the former being accompanied, as was the

Typical early Saxon cinerary urns with their distinctive patterning and decorative bulges. Excavated at Kettering.

norm, with weapons and in some cases drinking buckets, the women with a wide range of brooches, belt fittings, beads, pendants and keys. Many of the skeletons showed signs of rheumatism or severe arthritis. In another cemetery, uncovered at Wakerley during ironstone quarrying between 1968 and 1970, eight-five burials were found, all made within a relatively short time of each other. The dead were aged between one and forty-five years, and many were female. Once again, the usual grave goods for both sexes were in evidence, including a drinking horn. At both sites the burials dated from the late sixth and early seventh centuries.

Another intriguing find was made at Henslow Meadow near Aldwincle, a seemingly popular habitation/burial site since the Neolithic period, as we have already discussed. Close to the west abutment of a former Roman timber bridge over the Nene, and beneath the surface of the associated road (later known as Gartree Way), a skeleton was discovered with a seventh-century Saxon knife between its ribs – possibly a murder, or even a 'foundation sacrifice', an ancient practice carried out to protect a newly built structure from harm or to help the nearby community thrive. Superstition does not die easily in any society or in any age.

Even more remarkable was a major discovery by an amateur metal detectorist at Wollaston in 1997 during gravel extraction. It was a high-status mid-seventh-century helmet with a boar crest, nose guard and crescent-shaped cheek protectors (only one of two known examples in England). It belonged to a princely war leader whose remains were also found, together with a bowl and a richly-patterned steel sword in a wool-lined scabbard.

As the seventh century progressed and before Christianity was adopted, grave goods were becoming less common, probably in line with European fashion, and would eventually die out completely, as was the custom for Christian burials. In 1876, an interesting discovery was made at Desborough in a rectangular enclosure during ironstone quarrying. Among the forty roughly made burials on the site was the grave of a wealthy woman, containing a thirty-seven-piece gold-and-garnet-beaded necklace with a pendant gold cross. It perhaps accompanied her as part of a cautious 'hedging one's bets' situation during the transition from the old religion to the new. At the time of the discovery workmen had divided it among themselves, but it was retrieved, put back together and is now on display in the British Museum. There were other grave goods present, including two round-based amber tumblers, a brass pot, and a ladle.

And so, with the return of Christianity in the late seventh century, a standard form of burial evolved that became the norm and persists to this day. A typical early churchyard overlying a late-Saxon settlement was that which was excavated between 1971 and 1973 at Newton, near Geddington. This was made in order to determine the site and extent of the church and boundaries of St Leonard, which had slowly been demolished and built on after the parish of Great Newton merged with that of neighbouring Little Newton in 1440. Trial trenches managed to locate the position of the south wall of the churchyard, where twelve skeletons from the fourteenth century or earlier were discovered, two of which, touchingly, had their hand bones intertwined – united in death as they had been in life. Later, seventy-six skeletons were found, many of them children buried in cists (stone-lined graves). Towards the end of the dig in 1973, a priest was discovered buried in what would become the traditional manner for a cleric – with a surrogate patten and chalice.

As the centuries wore on, the purpose of the old burial sites was forgotten and although a great number of mounds were ploughed out or plundered, many were still held in awe, as if they had some supernatural connection. Round ones were deemed to belong to fairies, and long ones to giants or even dragons or some other powerful force that was not to be meddled with. Above all, they were believed to contain hoards of treasure. In 1527 a person appeared in court at Kettering, accused of demanding money for revealing where a precious hoard was hidden in such a mound. A superstitious element was implicit in his statement:

> … ther was iii thousand pounds of gold and sylver in a bank beside the crosse nygh hand to Kettering, and that it is in ii pottes within the ground. A man sprite and woman sprite do kepe teh said ii pottes.

3

FORMS OF BURIAL

EVOLUTION OF THE CHURCHYARD

After the Saxons adopted Christianity, and before churches became commonplace, it is likely that a preaching cross would have been erected at a specially chosen site, perhaps one with sacred significance for the community, by priests travelling from mother churches (minsters), many of which were on royal estates like Brigstock. The stumps or fragments of these crosses are frequently found today in churchyards, and some have been placed inside churches for preservation, such as the wheel cross-head at Mears Ashby, the two shafts at Nassington (one with carved interlacing, the other depicting a sun, moon and soldiers in part of a crucifixion scene), and a shaft with carved beasts and interlacing at Desborough. Others were recycled for the repair or rebuilding of the church fabric as part of an economy programme, as can be seen inside the towers of the churches at Lutton and Naseby.

These sites would act as burial places, the earliest desirable interments being as close as possible to the cross. After a church had been built, these would expand and evolve into churchyards. Some sites would be of particular appeal or significance to the newly converted, such as those with a circular or oval shape, which are usually of prehistoric origin, as is the case at Whittlebury. A hilltop siting such as that at Wadenhoe would have been seen as ideal, being that much closer to heaven. In other cases, a church may have been deliberately isolated from a settlement if built at a particularly sacred place such as a well or spring. Examples include the now-derelict church of St John the Baptist at Boughton Green, nearly three quarters of a mile from the village of Boughton, and the church of St Helen at Great Oxendon. (One must beware of such an assumption, however. The usual reason for isolation is more straightforward – a village may have been deserted, as was the case at Little Newton; or it may have moved away from the church as the settlement grew in size, such as Harrington, or for a more practical reason, such as to avoid flooding, as may have been the case with Stoke Albany.)

But what about those instances where an intended church site was abandoned in favour of a new one? This has happened all over Britain and, according to tradition, there were at least three such cases in the county. Repeated attempts at building the church of St Michael at the summit of a hill at Church Stowe (Stowe Nine Churches)

A typical thirteenth-century stone coffin lid with omega design and globular crosses.

were thwarted each time by the fabric being dismantled and tools taken away during the night by someone – or something – objecting to the work being carried out. According to one version of the tale, a monk volunteered to keep watch to find out the cause. He was startled by the sight of a 'hairy creature' dismantling the stonework at a great pace. As soon as the monk began to pray, the creature vanished, never to return, and the church was successfully completed. Similar circumstances are supposed to have occurred with the church of St Mary at Great Brington and the church of St James (formerly St Nicholas) at Syresham (the latter being built on the present site at Church Hill, which was long known locally as 'Church Hell'). In both cases the cause was never discovered, although it was long believed to be the work of disgruntled fairies. In these and other cases elsewhere, the legend is basically an allegory of the new religion supplanting the existing one.

From the twelfth century, some of the priests and early benefactors had specially made stone coffins that were sunk in the ground with their rims/upper edges level with the surface. They were usually either tapered or rectangular in shape, the inside of the latter being either a matching hollow (as in Roman times) or, more often, contoured for the body with a rounded hollow for the head, a good example of which can be seen at Warmington. They were fitted with a thick lid that was either flat or gently coped. Initially these were plain with no inscription, or perhaps a little decoration such as hatched diamonds (as at Easton on the Hill), but by the thirteenth century it was fashionable to decorate the whole lid with a variety of designs, the most common being those with a floriated cross at the top, a stepped cross base ('Calvary cross'

Medieval stone coffins in the
grounds of Peterborough Cathedral.

style) and/or four curving arms (the so-called 'omega design') in the centre, said either
to represent the ribbons that were suspended from a processional cross, or as a motif
based on those found on a bishop's mitre. Years later, a number of these lids would find
their way into churches when the churchyard was undergoing reorganisation for more
burial space, such as those at Nassington (eleven, ten of which are now fragmentary),
Woodnewton (three) and Rothwell. Others were taken into the porch and used as 'dole
stones', marking the place where annual charitable distributions took place (although,
alternatively, these might also take place at the grave site of the benefactor).

The coffins and remains, however, were disposed of elsewhere, although in some
cases a few coffins have survived and have been used for other purposes, for example
as a water trough for livestock, or for bedding flowers. Several of these survivors can
be found in the churchyards at Harringworth and Twywell (both near the gateways)
and Cotterstock (on the north side of the church), while a row of empty coffins stands
in the grounds of Peterborough Cathedral.

As the population grew during the medieval era, churchyards were not the kind
of tranquil places you see today. Many were unenclosed. It was quite normal to see
grazing animals disinterring corpses and bones. There would be games like 'fives' and
'single stick play', ballgames, fairs and markets, wrestling, dancing, sexual liaisons, and
later, perhaps, a cock pit. After the 1242 Assize of Arms and the 1285 First Statute of
Winchester came into force, all males of a certain 'rank' from the age of seven had to
be adept at archery. Henceforth arrows would be sharpened on the exterior walls of
a church, as can be seen at Fotheringhay or on a slab in the porch at Lowick; and no
doubt the churchyard was also used for practice. There were also seasonal mystery
plays acting out Biblical scenes, and miracle plays that re-enacted the lives of the saints,

the latter being replaced at a later date by morality plays depicting tussles between good and evil, or vice and virtue. One of the most popular plays in Northamptonshire was *The Wise and Foolish Virgins*, in which Christ consigns the wayward women to Hell. On the plus side, however, rent from stall holders at the markets, fairs and plays provided extra income for the parish, as did the brewing of communal parish 'ales', the proceeds of which were used to repair the church fabric or provide for the needy.

Following the Reformation, churchyards all around the county were commonly used as rubbish tips or sewage dumps. One particularly notable case was at Higham Ferrers, where it was recorded in 1637 that it was 'noysome as the people can scarce endure to passe thorow the church yarde by reason of the offensive sights and smells'.

At All Saints' in Northampton the same year, a survey reported 'the churchyard is basely defiled w[i]th excrements, and it appears there is the usuall evacuating ag[ains]t the church walls at the doors and at the most eminent ends and frontispieces therof'. Even long before the Reformation, such behaviour was a normal feature of life. At the church of St John in Peterborough, a payment of 4*d* was made in 1479 'for clensyng and carrying of ye yearth and muck out of the chyrchyerd about.'

WITHIN THE WALLS: INTRAMURAL BURIALS

As churches grew in size, it was inevitable that some of the more pious individuals, such as priests (if they had the means) and the wealthier members of the community, would want to be buried within the hallowed walls.

One way in which this could be done was in the form of an altar tomb, which was a stone, rectangular box-like structure topped with a ledger (a flat stone slab) that may have once been a shelter for a reliquary or the remains of a saint. This slab would hold the recumbent effigy of the deceased, who was buried beneath the floor.

EFFIGIES

Until the mid-fifteenth century, in common with all types of funerary monument including brasses, effigies would *not* show the likeness of the deceased. They would be chosen during a patron's lifetime from a range of images in a pattern book of the marbler/engraver. Figures were depicted on the altar tomb lying on their backs, some with hands on their chest or a sword, or clasped in prayer, and most often with outstretched legs, although there was a vogue for cross-legged images *c.* 1250–1350. Claims that the cross-legged deceased had been on a crusade is completely unfounded – it was purely a fashion device. Similarly, the men shown as knights had never necessarily been such, and most of the images were made long after the final Crusade of 1270–72. Other images were added for symbolic effect: a dog at the feet represented loyalty, while a lion at the feet represented valour.

Effigies were initially made of stone, either limestone (the first in the county being at Sudborough, depicting Robert de Vere *c.* 1250 – he *had* been a crusader), Purbeck

The sumptuous fifteenth-century alabaster altar tomb of Sir Ralph and Lady Katherine Greene at Lowick.

marble (the first in the county being that of Sir David de Esseby at Castle Ashby, *c.* 1268), Barnack rag (at Brixworth), red sandstone (Braunston, Ashton, Woodford Halse), clunch (Warkworth, Marholm and Great Brington, where eight of the ten monuments of the Spencer family are of this fabric) and alabaster (an ideal 'soft' stone for carving, which made its first appearance in the county in 1371 at Spratton with the tomb of Sir John Swinford). Alabaster would come to dominate much of the funerary market until marble became the most fashionable material for sculpture from the seventeenth century onwards. The best alabaster was quarried around the Chellaston area of Derbyshire, and it was from here that one of the finest tombs of its kind anywhere was commissioned and made for Sir Ralph Greene (*d.* 1419) by his wife, Katherine, at a cost of £40. This sum included gilding and painting, and a copy of the agreement/indenture still survives. This impressive monument, now without a canopy, stands between the chancel and north chapel in the church of St Peter at Lowick and depicts the couple lying together hand in hand – an extremely rare feature in funerary art. He is in armour, she is in a long mantle and wearing an elaborate winged headdress. Some traces of the original colouring are still visible in places.

Single female effigies are somewhat less common, the best example of which is at Dodford, depicting Wentiliana de Keynes (1376). Others can be found at Irthlingborough (*c.* 1490), Gayton, Woodford Halse, Eydon, Crick, and Barnack. Inside the tower of the church at Cotterstock is the fourteenth-century figure of a woman,

The wooden effigy of Sir William de Combermartyne, *c.* 1318, in the nave of the church of St Margaret at Alderton.

depicted in relief with only the upper half of the body showing, the rest being left blank or covered. A singular late example dating from 1620 can be seen at Church Stowe; a true likeness of the deceased is carved in black-and-white marble. (A full list of stone effigies in the county may be found in the appendices of this book.)

In addition, wooden effigies were popular *c.* 1250–1350. They were carved from selected pieces of oak with a minimum width of 2 feet (60 cm), which would be hollowed out on the underside to prevent cracking, with any surface imperfections like knots concealed by being glued with linen. A thin coat of gusso (parchment size and whitening agent) for priming the surface was applied, followed by a thicker coat where decoration was to be made in relief (i.e. raised surface features), or on those larger areas where gilding and silvering were to be added. Then, after using the same method as for painting stone using tempera (a form of distemper where colour pigments are dissolved in water and mixed with a binder such as size/glue), the task was completed by adding a coat of an oil-based varnish.

Many wooden effigies are cross-legged, like their stone counterparts. Such a fashionable device would also have had a practical advantage in strengthening the reduced thickness of a more vulnerable material such as wood in that part of the image. Again, like stone images, they would originally have been brightly painted, but have since lost their colouring through age, neglect, damp and temperature changes. Today there are few wooden effigies left in England, but Northamptonshire has eleven

The stone cross-legged effigy of Robert de Vere in a funerary recess at Sudborough.

of them – including three double effigies of husband and wife. Another is recorded at Spratton, where it lay on top of the alabaster tomb of Sir John Swinford (*d.* 1376). The survivors are:

- Ashton (near Roade): Sir Philip le Lou (1315)
- Gayton: Sir Philip de Gayton and his wife (1316)*
- Woodford: Sir William and Eleanor (Alionara) de Traylli (1290/1316)*
- Alderton: Sir William de Combemartyne (1318)
- Dodford: Hawise de Keynes (1329)
- Braybrooke: Thomas de Latymer (1334)
- Paulerspury: Sir Lawrence de Paveley and his wife (1340/1346)* (The base is a later replacement.)
- Cold Higham: Sir John de Pateshull (1350)

*double effigies

There was also a fashion for recumbent 'demi-figure' effigies during the same period, particularly of priests. Only the upper half of the body was depicted, the lower half being covered in some way or left blank. (The term 'demi-figure' is also used for a later, different form of monument, discussed below.) There are examples in the south chapel of the church of St Mary at Geddington, and at Weston by Welland, where the monument is partially obscured by the church organ, while at Great Brington there is a brass depicting the demi-figure of a priest, John de Clipston (1344).

Perhaps the most unique form of altar tomb, however, is the 'cadaver tomb'. These were for high-ranking prelates such as archbishops and abbots and were fashionable in England for a short period, 1420–80. Good examples can be seen in the cathedrals at Canterbury and Lincoln. They were two-tier structures, the upper level showing the deceased in his priestly robes, beneath which is a likeness of his rotting corpse. They were meant to show the inevitability and appearance of death, and were intended as a lesson in humility – i.e. everyone, whatever their station in life, will end up the same way. The sole example in Northamptonshire can be found in the former chantry chapel of the church of St Lawrence at Towcester. It is that of Archdeacon Sponne, who was rector of the church from 1442 until his death in 1448. Interestingly, when the monument was moved from its original site in 1835, his skeleton was found resting on a bed of white sand in an excellent state of preservation, albeit with no trace of his vestments. After a few hours exposure to the air, however, the remains disintegrated. Such a situation is not unknown (see below).

An alternative method of housing the effigy would be the tomb recess, or funerary arch. Many of these, now mostly empty, can be found set into the walls of the north or south aisles of the county's churches, although some were external (such as those at Brigstock, Stanion and Northampton Holy Sepulchre). As many as four recesses can be found in a church (as at Watford). Most of the effigies have long since vanished, one in particular, that of Johannes de Ros (*d.* 1377), suffering a particularly ignominious fate when it was removed in 1790 because the wife of the vicar of Stoke Albany found it 'black and hideous'. It was initially turned over and used as a seat, before finally being broken into pieces and buried under the church footpath.

Tomb recesses should not be confused with Easter sepulchres, which have an identical arch-like appearance. Unlike the tomb recesses, they were always situated on the *north* side of the chancel, beside the altar. As the name suggests, Easter sepulchres played an important role during the Easter period, when a lighted candle and a cross would be placed on the surface, and a vigil was maintained by a team of villagers on a rota system from Good Friday until Easter Sunday. You will see them inside the churches at Twywell, Lutton, Grendon and Marston St Lawrence. However, most of the churches in the county did not have 'permanent' Easter sepulchres – they were not usually part of the church fabric. Instead, they were transportable, in the form of a wooden frame adorned with drapery and painted wooden panels, and were brought out specifically at that time. They were such an important feature that money or goods were often given in bequests and wills for their upkeep or repair, for example:

- 'I bequeath to the mendyng of the sepulchre and the light there, xxd.' (J. Abron of Wadenhoe, 1526)
- 'I bequeath ten ewes for maykyng a sepulcher.' (Thomas Hunt of Cransley, 1516)
- 'To the sepulchre, vjs. viijd. in money, or catell.' (John Bull of Great Oakley, *c.* 1526)

The fifteenth-century cadaver tomb of Archdeacon Sponne at Towcester.

Although not the norm, it is possible in some cases that the more 'permanent' Easter sepulchres *could* also act as tomb recesses, as at Stoke Albany, Corby, Wakerley, Cogenhoe, Watford, Flore and Sudborough. Although unusual, this could happen if the right kind of influence was exerted and sufficient money changed hands – and what a sense of glory the devout individual would have had – the ultimate burial – lying next to the altar, in the most sacred part of the church, where the holy image was placed annually.

The use of Easter sepulchres and bequests, like many other aspects of traditional religious ceremony, died out during the Reformation.

SUBTERRANEAN BURIALS

For many of those with the means who did want to be buried within the confines of the church building – ideally as close to the altar as possible – there was one popular choice: beneath the floor. For many years, until stone slabs or even wooden blocks were used, the floor would be of beaten earth, sometimes mixed with ox blood for cohesion, and strewn with rushes, sweet-smelling plants and herbs. In the course of time, some of these grave plots would be extended further and deeper under the chancel, often into the nave or in a side chapel/transept, and become family vaults or crypts.

The desire to be buried in this way, some in a spectacular fashion, appears in many pre-Reformation bequests, including the following examples:

- '... a black bullock on condition I lay within the chancel'. (John Nichols, Islip, 1531)
- '... to be buried in the chapel of the church [of All Saints]'. (John Page, draper, Northampton, 1501)
- '... to be buried in the church of seynt Andrew the Apostle before the Trynyte'. (Mary Cotton, Brigstock, 1521)
- '... to be buried before the image of the blessyd Trinite'. (Richard Garen, Stanion, 1541)
- '... to be buried in the chauncell of Thyngdon afore my deske there'. (W. Stokys, vicar, Finedon, 1540)
- '... to be buryed in the chancel of Oundell, if I die there, with an honest stone to cover me, and that my body be buried immediately after my death and that 5 candles of wax – and no more – be placed round my body in the form of a cross'. (Richard de Treton, Oundle, 1393, translated from Latin)
- '... to be buryed in the tumbe of marbull that I have ordeyned under the north wall of the chapel of holy Trinite in the parish chyrche of Norton aforesaid'. (Richard Mydelton, Greens Norton, 1489)
- '... to the high altar of the church where I shall be buried, 4 torches, each torch weighing 10 pounds ... The testator is unwilling that any of the said torches should be lighted in any other way about his wretched body'. (John de Newenham, Newnham, 1369, translated from Latin)

Many of these plots had a stone slab (ledger) set in the floor with the name, age and date of death of the deceased. This was a popular form of grave marker for years to come, and there are a great many to be found around the county, although few survive from before the seventeenth century. The only early examples are at Oundle (1278), Lowick (1415), Geddington (1480), East Carlton (1583) and Weldon (1586). The largest number of seventeenth-century ledgers can be found at Paulerspury, Sudborough, Aldwincle All Saints, and Yarwell.

Some of these ledgers make clear the large number of premature deaths that occurred in past centuries – especially infant deaths. A typical example is at Wakerley, where four sons of the 3rd Earl of Exeter died in 1636 and 1638 at the ages of two, seven, eight and ten.

One can imagine the effect of multiple burials at such close proximity to those members of the congregation present in the church above. The smell of decay and putrefaction of the dead would permeate the soil and fill the air. This would have been a common problem for most churches, even after wooden floors replaced the standard beaten earth, and there were often references to this problem and the action that had to be taken, such as at Paulerspury in 1827, when the churchwardens were asked to 'lay down a stone slab without air holes', due to the stench from the vault below.

Some burials were covered in a layer (or were placed on a bed) of charcoal, which may or may not have acted as a form of deodorant or in some kind of preservative capacity, the latter being of great importance for the Day of Judgment. It was a practice occasionally carried out with some high-status burials in the late Saxon era until the latter part of the eleventh century. Some interesting discoveries have been made during maintenance work in churches. In 1869, while levelling the surface of the floor in the church of All Saints at Rushton, workmen lifted up one of the uneven flagstones in the chancel and found a large space filled with powdered charcoal, beneath which they found the perfectly preserved body of a young female. However, after having been in anaerobic (oxygen-free) conditions for centuries, the body crumbled into powder. A similar discovery, albeit without charcoal, was made at the church of St Edmund at Warkton in 1930, where the underground heating system was being overhauled. Workmen uncovered a wooden coffin, within which, once again, there was the perfectly preserved body of another young female with long hair. She was believed to be from a much later era, possibly the sixteenth century. It was promptly resealed and subsequently reburied.

Worse still was another problem that would accumulate through the centuries. The practice of internal burial of several generations could weaken the church fabric, leading to a potentially dangerous situation. This was fairly common, especially where one particular area of the church was over-used. The worst recorded case was at the church of St Mary Magdalene at Yarwell in 1782, when snow and rain caused the coping of the nave to fall on the roof of an aisle – the result of burials repeatedly being made too close to the walls and lower section of the foundations. Both aisles were consequently removed for safety reasons. Similarly, in 1850, at the church of St Michael in Haselbech, the north aisle was found to be unstable due to erosion of the floor level – again caused by burials being made too close to the structure over the years. Repairs were consequently carried out to both aisles between 1856 and 1858, albeit without necessitating their removal, as had been the case at Yarwell.

Some of these wealthy individuals would have been buried in lead coffins, a notable example being that of Cecily Neville, the Duchess of York and mother of Edward IV, who lived at Fotheringhay for a number of years before moving to another York family estate. On her death, she was brought back to the village and buried beside her husband 'under the quire' of the church. Another royal individual with a briefer connection with the village was Mary, Queen of Scots, who was imprisoned there before being executed in February 1587. The body was subsequently embalmed and remained in the village until July, when it was carried by torchlight procession late at night to Peterborough Cathedral, accompanied by heralds.[*] After a special service had been conducted by the

---

[*] It should be noted that night-time burials were not particularly unusual, being mainly for suicides, unbaptised children and members of the aristocracy.

Bishop (which was attended by distinguished guests), the body was interred in a lead coffin near Henry VIII's first wife, Catherine of Aragon, who had been buried there in 1535. The event was portrayed in an early twentieth-century work, *Tales of Mermaid Tavern* by Alfred Noyes (1880–1958):

> The witch from over the water,
> The fay from over the foam,
> The bride from Edinburgh's town,
> With satin shoes and silken gown,
> A queen and a great king's daughter,
> Thus they carried her home.
>
> With torches and with scutcheons,
> Unhonoured and unseen,
> With the lilies of France, in the wind a-stir,
> And the Lion of Scotland over her,
> Darkly in the dead of night,
> They carried the queen to the queen.

The body remained there for twenty-five years, at which time Mary's son, James I of England, ordered her remains to be disinterred and transferred to Henry VII's chapel in Westminster Abbey. Both grave sites were later ransacked by Parliamentarian troops, who pulled down the protective railings and some of the funerary furnishings during the English Civil War.

The thirteenth-century crypt under the south transept at the church of St Peter at Oundle was certainly used at one stage for burials, but is now empty; it has dangerously worn steps and is filled with rubble. Its beautifully ribbed vaulted roofing contains an image of the foliate Green Man looking down – a symbol of resurrection and protection. It would have been used not for any manorial family but probably for important clerics and may have had some connection with St Wilfred, the renowned early English Bishop of York, who died in 709 in the town in where he had earlier founded a monastery. His remains were taken to Ripon Cathedral, where they lie today. Perhaps the later church held a reliquary or item belonging to the saint that was displayed for pilgrims to the crypt (although there is no recorded evidence for this). There is another ribbed, vaulted crypt under the chancel of the church of St Andrew at Harlestone.

Long-disused vaults and crypts have been sealed or blocked up and are usually inaccessible nowadays, although the entrances to some are still highly visible, such as the Dolben vault at Finedon, the Tryon vault at Harringworth (with railings and steps), and the external Lyveden vault at Brigstock. Other indications of hidden vaults include large rings in some of the floor ledgers, as at Blatherwycke. A few have been cleared of their contents, as at Weldon, and used for modern purposes, such as the storage of maintenance machinery for the churchyard.

At Badby, when a brick vault was being made by the Revd Thomas Cox for his family in 1786, a skull was found with its beard still intact. He believed it was one of his seventeenth-century predecessors. The new vault was completed just in time by the vicar, for his twin daughters died that year, followed two years later by his wife and son.

BRASSES

The vogue for funerary brasses in England began in the thirteenth century. Sheets of latten (an alloy of two-thirds copper and one-third zinc with a small quantity of tin or lead) were imported from Germany, and became known as brasses. The sheets would be divided into small panels that would then be inscribed by a 'marbler' (mason/brass engraver), using a design chosen from a pattern book by the patron in his/her lifetime. Like funerary effigies, the final product would *not* be the likeness of the deceased. Examples of this can be seen at Cransley and Raunds, where both couples depicted are identical. Initially the main centres for engraving were Norwich, London, York and Bristol. One such London-based marbler, William West, came from the county and is actually depicted with his parents and siblings on a brass in the north transept of the church of All Saints at Sudborough. He can be seen standing between his father, also named William (*d*. 1390), and his mother, Joan (now headless). The brass dates from *c*. 1430 and may well be his work.

Like masons and some glaziers and woodcarvers, a number of marblers left some form of quality control or signature on their completed work. Only two brasses with this feature are known to survive in England, and one of these appears on the life-size effigy of Lawrence St Maur at Higham Ferrers (the other is in Cambridgeshire). It is in the form of a circular mark, within which is a back-to-front 'N' surmounted by a hammer with a six-point star on either side.

Although expensive at first, their chief advantage was that they took up less room at a time when floor space for the larger monuments and early ledgers was becoming increasingly limited. Their other purpose was to act as a source for prayers from passers-by, which, in line with pre-Reformation religious thinking, would help ease the soul's journey through Purgatory.

Today there are around 4,000 brasses left in England, Northamptonshire having 241 survivors, 102 of which are 'pictorial' and 139 with an inscription only (often in Latin). They can be found in three forms: on walls, on altar tombs, and in floors. Some of the latter are now concealed under a carpet for extra protection. In addition, there are several indents of former brasses that have been lost, stolen or damaged (many during the Reformation and Civil War), as at Courteenhall, Oundle, Fotheringhay, Irthlingborough, Wakerley, Blatherwycke, Warmington, more recently at Brampton Ash, and on the external wall at Kingscliffe. Thirty-two of these date from the thirteenth century, sixteen from the fourteenth century, and four from the sixteenth century. Others have parts missing, as at Burton Latimer, Blatherwycke, Sudborough and Naseby. Some of the surviving brasses are palimpsests, a more economical way of commemorating the deceased person via the recycling of an existing brass by using the reverse side for engraving (as at Easton Neston). Some of these would have come from dissolved monastic houses after 1538.

Here lieth Jone furnace the wife of James furnace
that was and is not: saying to them that reads this:
you are and shall not be: Who in my life tyme
trusted to haue a dwelling place in heauen wt
god the father and in glorye eke to rayngne wt
Christ his sonne. A°. Dm̄ .1585. dw 21.Junn.

The brass of Jane Furnace, 1585, now under carpet in the central aisle at Church Brampton.

When the patron died, the brass would not be placed in the church straight away: some time would normally elapse until (in the case of husband and wife) the decease of both partners, at which time additional wording or imagery would sometimes be added to the date(s) of death, as requested by a member of the family. Then it was either affixed to a wall (usually in the chancel), or to the side or top of an existing monument, with brass rivets. When the floor was used, a shallow depression was made in the surface and the brass was embedded in pitch before being secured with the rivets.

The earliest surviving brasses in the county are of priests: at Higham Ferrers (Lawrence St Maur, *d.* 1337), with arcading, depictions of saints, and an angel holding a soul in a cloth; and at Rothwell (William de Rothwell, *d.* 1361), with angels by the pillow of the deceased. Thereafter brasses include male figures in military or civil dress, including the members of the newly emerging middle classes, such as merchants or scholars like Thomas Hurland (1589), the 'schoolmaster' at Fotheringhay. The first brass depicting a husband and wife together is also at Higham Ferrers (*c.* 1400), in this case the father and mother of Archbishop Chichele. And in an age where life expectancy was short, even more so for women giving birth, it is no surprise to see a man depicted with two or more wives, as at Naseby (1446) and Welford (1585). The most unique brass of a couple is that of Sir Walter Mauntell (*c.* 1487) and his wife at Nether Heyford, in which they are depicted holding hands – a rare show of affection in funerary art. The brass is also unusual in that the engraver has mistakenly inscribed the

A standard sixteenth-century brass depicting William Lane and his wife (1502, Orlingbury).

date as 'mcccclxxxixii' instead of 'mcccclxxxvii', perhaps due to lack of a firm grasp of Latin numerals – or so it is thought.

Women began to appear with their husbands for the first time in the late fourteenth century. Like their husbands, their hands would be clasped in prayer. Occasionally during the next century they would be depicted with their hands outspread, their thumbs forming a 'W' pattern – although there are no known examples of this kind in Northamptonshire.

As was the case with effigies, women could be depicted by themselves. There are a fair number around the county, the earliest surviving images being at Warkworth, where there are two: Margaret Brownynge (*d.* 1420) and Lady Chetwode (*d.* 1430). These are followed chronologically by those at Higham Ferrers (Edith Chauncellor, the image of who, like some others, is now headless, *c.* 1467), Newnham (Letitia Catesby, *d.* 1499); Wappenham (Constance Butler, *d.* 1506); Collyweston (Elizabeth Follett, *d.* 1508); Flore (Alyce Wyrley, d. 1537); Dingley (Anne Boroeghe, *d.* 1577); Barton Seagrave (Jane Floyde, *d.* 1616); and Dodford (Bridget Wyrley, *d.* 1637).

Unmarried women were depicted with their hair hanging loose or uncovered (although occasionally married women or widows were shown in such a manner). Women sworn to chastity were usually depicted in a thin, veiled headdress, cordon and belt.

Like the funerary effigies, brasses give us a glimpse of changing fashion styles through the ages. Priests would be depicted in various types of robes and garments such as the alb, stole, amice, cope and maniple, often holding a chalice and patten in their hands. In the case of other male figures, it should be noted that wearing armour did not necessarily denote that the person was a knight – again, like the face of the deceased, armour was something chosen from a range of figures in the pattern book, which functioned like a modern clothing catalogue. The earliest images would show a moustached or bearded figure in chain mail and hood, usually with a sword and shield. During the fourteenth century plate armour for different parts of the body and new styles of helmet were being developed, and by the end of that century, it was possible to protect the whole body with jointed armour – which was consequently depicted in funerary sculpture and brasses. Hair, where shown, was fashionably long until the 1400s, when shorter hair, beards and moustaches became the norm, and by the end of that century it was customary to be clean-shaven.

Fashion-wise, the brasses present a more compelling and comprehensive view of changing styles of women's clothing through time than their male counterparts. In the period 1050–1490 fashion was slow to change, with alterations to existing styles being the norm in most cases. The basic medieval garment for a woman of higher status was a loose-fitting gown (worn over a kirtle with narrow sleeves) with a wimple (a long piece of linen or silk) draped around the neck, drawn up around the chin, and fastened above the ears. It was the type of headdress, however, that changed the most – it evolved from a veil resting on the shoulders, or a coverchief with headband, until the late fourteenth century and the appearance of the open hood, the steeple headdress (a tall stiff cone covered in a long veil), and the ram's horn headdress. During the next century, the butterfly headdress came into fashion. It was made up of a wire framework supporting a gauze veil spread out on each side of the head. The early years of the sixteenth century saw the introduction of the gable, English and French hoods. The tall hat appeared in the following century.

Groups of children began to be depicted with their parents in the early years of the fifteenth century and thereafter brasses make a great contribution to the medieval genealogical record of these families, filling in gaps until the introduction of parish registers during the Reformation. Girls were often shown beneath or behind their mothers. The first known brass depicting children with their parents is at Ashby St Ledger and dates from 1416.

One of the largest brasses can be seen on the north side of the round nave of the church of the Holy Sepulchre in Northampton – a huge vertical panel showing George Coles (*d.* January 1640) with his two wives, Sarah (*d.* 1607) on his right and Eleanor (*d.* 1631) on his left. Both women wear the then-fashionable tall hats. There is an inscription around the border detailing Coles' yearly charity to the poor, and his twelve children are shown in two small panels, side by side, beneath the image of the parents. Beneath this are two clasped hands, and another panel inscribed:

Farewell, true Friend, Reader understand by this mysterious Knott of Hand in Hand, this Emblem doth (what Friends fayle to doe) repair our Friendshipp and its Firmness toe, such was our Love, not Time but Death doth sever our mortall Parts, but our immortal never, all Things doe vanish here belowe, above such as our Life is there, such is our Love.

Appearances can be deceptive. Some brasses look genuinely medieval but are later creations. In the north chapel of the church of St James the Apostle at Grafton Underwood is a remarkable medieval-looking brass set into a large marble slab, which the Wilson Fitzpatrick children commissioned from the renowned pioneering Gothic Revival architect and designer Augustus Pugin in 1841, in honour of their half-sister, Lady Gertrude Fitzpatrick, who had died earlier that year. In the chancel of the church of St Nicholas at Islip there is a 1467 brass depicting the merchant John Nichol and his wife Agnys. However, this is a recreation of the original, carried out in 1911 by the Bedfordshire clergyman Revd Hubert Macklin (1866–1917), who had been asked by American descendants of the family to organise the task. He was the author of a definitive text on brasses, *The Brasses of England* (Methuen, 1907), and a founder of the Memorial Brass Society in 1887. A descendant of the Nichol family had settled in the American colonies in 1664 and became honorary governor of New York. An area of Long Island was eventually purchased by him and a town established. It was named Islip in honour of his roots. Contact is made between the two settlements today.

The churches with the greatest number of brasses are Higham Ferrers with nine, followed by Ashby St Ledger, Wappenham and Warkworth, which have five apiece. Sizes of brasses around the county vary from as little as 5 inches (13 cm) – usually those with an inscription only – to 5 feet 3 inches (1.6 m) at Castle Ashby. A list of surviving illustrated brasses can be found in the appendices, and their imagery is further discussed in Chapter 6.

POST-REFORMATION MONUMENTS

In the years following the Reformation there was a new religious outlook, an obsession for more physical reminders of the dead to replace chantries and church bequests, and the rise of the meritocracy – self-made men (with names like Spencer, Cecil, Knightley, Brudenell, Montagu and Cave) who had accumulated wealth and status through commercial interests or risen to high office in a legal or administrative capacity under successive Tudor governments. All of this led to the appearance of more sumptuous, expensive funerary monuments and, in some cases, the setting up of family chapels, many of which would continue in use until the closing years of the nineteenth century. A visit to the churches at Great Brington, Stanford and Fawsley, for example, will give some idea of the opulence and sense of grandeur achieved.

It was during this period that 'portrait effigies' came into being. For the first time, the deceased was depicted based on a real-life portrait. Two good examples of this can be seen – one at Fawsley on the 1534 alabaster tomb of Sir Richard Knightley and his wife Joan, and one at Stamford St Martin, that of William Cecil (Lord Burghley), the former Chief Minister, who held the staff of Lord High Treasurer and died in 1599.

Altar tombs – either free-standing or against a wall – would continue to appear until well into the nineteenth century (such as that of Baron Lyveden at Brigstock, 1876), some with the addition of a canopy and symbolic figures. One of the most remarkable is the 1621 tomb of Sir Anthony and Lady Grace Mildmay at Apethorpe. Considered

One of the most sumptuous
seventeenth-century monuments
in England – the Mildmay tomb at
Apethorpe.

to be one of the finest of its kind in England, it is a huge monument of black and white
marble under a huge domed canopy.

During this time a new form of memorial appeared and soon became popular: the
wall monument (also known as a hanging monument, or mural monument). The
larger form could be ornate but without effigies (as at Braybrooke, Little Oakley
and Fotheringhay – all sixteenth century). Later, they appeared in a more detailed
form, with obituaries and funerary verse, some with open doors, as at East Carlton
(Sir Geoffrey Palmer and his wife, *c*. 1673), and some with panels, as on the obelisk
monument of the infant Henry Montagu (*d*. 1625) at the now-truncated church of
Barnwell All Saints.

The more common form, however, was smaller, brightly coloured and depicted whole
families – the husband and wife in contemporary dress, facing each other in profile
across a prayer desk, hands clasped in prayer, with their children ranged below them,
sons on one side, daughters on the other. There are good examples – many of which
have retained their original colouring – at Oundle, Bulwick, Rushden and Brampton
Ash. Sometimes only one person was depicted, looking outwards towards the observer,
as at Clipston (the merchant George Buswell, with his hands on a book, *d*. 1632),
Broughton (the rector, Robert Bolton, with his hands on a bible, *d*. 1631) and Barnwell
St Andrew. The latter depicts the benefactor and cleric Nicholas Latham (*d*. 1620) at a

A post-Reformation hanging wall monument to the Morgan family (*c.* 1560, Nether Heyford).

reading desk. At Lutton, a 1633 wall monument shows three members of the manorial Apreece family looking outwards (Robert, William and Robert – father, grandfather and great grandfather respectively of Hieronimus Apreece, who had commissioned the memorial). A different member of the family, Adlard, is shown on another wall monument nearby, kneeling at prayer, but in profile. Similarly, in the same posture at Marston Trussell there is the image of Mark Brewster (*d.* 1612), a merchant and adventurer who was later executed in Moscow for piracy.

Hanging monuments could reach great proportions in height – such as the arched Yelverton memorial (1631) at Easton Maudit, which depicts the semi-reclining figure of the husband in the foreground with his wife on a platform above and behind him, and a tall caryatid on either side.

The seventeenth century saw the introduction of the most popular form of memorial of all, one which would continue to be in use until recent times: the wall tablet. More economical than hanging monuments but just as effective, they could range from a small rectangular panel with basic details about the deceased (name, age, date of death, and relationships) to something larger and more ornate with an architectural framework, obelisks, pediments, pilasters, cartouches, scrolls, lozenges, ovals and more. There are countless examples inside every church around the county, often made of white marble, while there are sometimes examples in slate and limestone on the exterior walls of churches, such as those at Weldon, Marston Trussell and Thrapston.

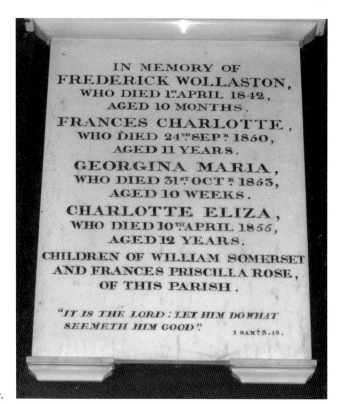

IN MEMORY OF
FREDERICK WOLLASTON,
WHO DIED 1ST APRIL 1842,
AGED 10 MONTHS.
FRANCES CHARLOTTE,
WHO DIED 24TH SEPT 1850,
AGED 11 YEARS.
GEORGINA MARIA,
WHO DIED 31ST OCT R 1853,
AGED 10 WEEKS.
CHARLOTTE ELIZA,
WHO DIED 10TH APRIL 1855,
AGED 12 YEARS.
CHILDREN OF WILLIAM SOMERSET
AND FRANCES PRISCILLA ROSE,
OF THIS PARISH.

*"IT IS THE LORD : LET HIM DO WHAT
SEEMETH HIM GOOD."* 1 SAM: 3.18.

A typical wall tablet in the
church of St Andrew, Cransley.

One of the most interesting is to Thomas Randolph, the poet and playwright who led a dissolute life in London, but who died at the age of twenty-four during a visit to the county in 1640. It was commissioned by his friend Sir Christopher Hatton, at a cost of £10 – a considerable sum for the time, and was made by the leading London-based sculptor and Master Mason to the Crown, Nicholas Stone (1585–1647). It incorporates a sixteen-line epitaph set within an oval surrounded by a laurel wreath. Another interesting example, at Wadenhoe, has a poignant inscription to Thomas Welch Hunt and his wife Caroline, 'who were both cruelly shot by banditti' while on honeymoon in Italy in December 1824. They died from the wounds they sustained.

HATCHMENTS

Until the seventeenth century, it was customary for the helmet and other pieces of armour or weaponry belonging to a deceased lord of the manor to be taken in procession to the church, where they were displayed. Known as 'achievements', some of these still exist – albeit rusted with time – in the churches at Apethorpe, Barnwell All Saints, Braybrooke, Canons Ashby, Great Brington, Higham Ferrers, Paulerspury and Steane. Not to be confused with these, however, are pieces of armour from elsewhere, such as at Raunds, and items from the English Civil War at Naseby and Ravensthorpe.

The successor to this was the 'hatchment', which originated in the Low Countries during the sixteenth century. They are recognisable by their diamond shape as opposed to royal coats of arms, which are normally rectangular. Confusingly, there are rare cases in England where the latter can also be diamond-shaped, as in the church of All Saints at Easton on the Hill. Several churches have both types of furnishings, e.g. Marston Trussell (the chancel and south aisle), Wadenhoe (both now in the bell ringing chamber) and the redundant church of Aldwincle All Saints (where they hang side by side in the north aisle).

Interestingly, a predecessor to these existed during the fifteenth century in Europe. They were in the form of 'escutcheons', small square panels of *living* knights, depicting their coats of arms. One example is that of the English king Edward IV (1442–92) at Bruges, which lies in a region where he had sought temporary sanctuary during the Wars of the Roses. They are connected with the Order of the Golden Fleece, a chivalric order established on the model of the Order of the Garter by Philip of Burgundy in 1430 that consisted of twenty-four members. If the escutcheon was depicted with a cord or belt tied or hanging at the top and had the inscription 'Trespasse', it meant the knight was deceased.

Although the display of hatchments did not really take hold in England until well into the seventeenth century, there are at least two precursors in the county with similar features. The first is now displayed in the chancel of the church of St Michael and All Angels at Great Oakley and dates from 1638. It is rectangular in form, depicting a coat of arms on a black background. It is that of Thomas Brooke, who was lord of the manor from 1620 until his death, and is a rare example of a painted funerary monument with a manorial coat of arms, but without standard hatchment features – one half would have been painted white, since his wife, Jane, survived him by another two years. It is, however, a lucky survival, for when the church was being reorganised to accommodate a new organ the hatchment had to be removed from its original site. It could have been destroyed, but thanks to one far-sighted member of the congregation it has not suffered the fate of many hatchments.

The second precursor hangs in the north aisle of the church at Barnwell St Andrews. Dating from 1665, it is a small, diamond-shaped panel with a black-and-gold background on which is depicted a coat of arms and a lengthy inscription in English and Latin. Around the edges are the images of bones, a skull and an hourglass. It is a funerary monument to Elizabeth Worthington, who was the daughter of the rector serving the church at the time, and who, like so many young people of the time, died in the prime of her life.

The earliest known standard type of hatchment, however, is at the other end of the county, at Easton Neston. Because of its remarkable condition, the authenticity of its age (1690) was once questioned. It was considered a replacement of the original.

Hatchments remained popular until the end of the nineteenth century. Three later examples appeared in the county, the last of which was that of Lord Brooke, former chairman of Northamptonshire County Council, who died at Great Oakley at 1944.

They were usually placed over the entrance of the manorial home for a set period as a sign of mourning before being transferred to the church, where they were usually hung on the wall of one of the aisles, and were often accompanied with a Latin (sometimes

A standard type of hatchment, one of three hanging in the church of St Mary at Weedon Lois.

French) motto, the most common being 'Resurgum' ('I shall rise again'), 'Mors janua vitae' ('Death is everlasting life'), 'Mors nih' ('Death is my gain'), 'In coelo quies' ('I rest in heaven') and 'Spes mea deus' ('God is my hope'). There are also two rare cases where the motto is in English: at Everdon ('Patience and perseverance') and at Welton Place ('In Christ is my hope').

By the time the county historian and antiquarian Christopher Markham (1859–1937) had completed his survey of hatchments in 1910, many had already disappeared. They were either victims of Victorian church restoration or had been destroyed in other circumstances. The redundant church at Fawsley was among those where several were once recorded. Since the last survey in the early 1970s, others have been found (for example at Wadenhoe), while at least sixteen listed by Markham are known to have been lost (two have been sold). This number will inevitably increase as the hatchments become more fragile, as is the case at Haselbech and Rushton, where efforts have been made to give some measure of protection against further damage. Great Oakley formerly had six, but the first to be hung in the church (Sir Richard de Capell Brooke, *d.* 1830) fell down and, to avoid further damage, was removed to the hall. There are currently 153 surviving hatchments, a list of which can be found in the appendices.

To identify which partner has died, the first step is to look at the background. If it is all black, both spouses are deceased. If one half is white, there is a surviving partner, and to work out if it is male or female you should imagine you are behind the hatchment, as if holding a shield. The female side is always to your left ('sinister'), the male to the right ('dexter'). Although not dated, hatchments also give useful manorial information via the central coat of arms, which is usually divided into sections (or 'quarters') for each of the families united by marriage. An all-black background with a simple coat of arms ('without quarters') will tell you that the deceased was unmarried.

On some hatchments, there are pairs of supporters, each holding one side of the coat of arms, similar to the lion and the unicorn on the royal coat of arms. These were usually 'wildmen', a form of Green Man depicted wielding a club, branch, tree or banner, representing strength, protection and fertility. Such a device was common on the coats of arms of noble families and was a symbolic means of guarding the bloodline – ensuring the succession of male heirs would continue the family name for posterity. They can be found on the coats of arms of royal houses, such as those of Denmark and former Prussia. In Northamptonshire they can be seen on hatchments at Haselbech and Weedon Lois. The image also appears on an eighteenth-century altar tomb at Yarwell.

THE EIGHTEENTH CENTURY AND BEYOND

The eighteenth century saw a fashion for large, ornately sculptured, standing monuments that were set against the wall or placed in alcoves. Highly expensive, they reflected the Rococo style, a good number of examples being produced by three renowned sculptors: Louis Roubiliac (1702–62) at Southwick and Warkton, Michael Rysbrack (1694–1770) at Stoke Doyle, and Peter Scheemakers (1691–1781) at Rockingham. Rococo had developed from the heavy, dramatic and emotional features of the Baroque style of the previous century. In comparison, it was frivolous, airy, blissful, intimate, playful and somewhat idyllic – an artificial style brought to life in marble with pastel colours and whiteness, curving images, cherubs, nymphs, gods and goddesses.

However, it was the Neoclassical style of the 1750s and beyond that saw the supreme use of marble in funerary monuments. Best seen in the work of Joseph Nollekens (1737–1823) at Great Brington and Whiston, and Sir Richard Westmacott (1775–1856), whose work can be seen at Grafton Underwood and Marston St Lawrence and whose father and son were also accomplished sculptors, the style was influenced by what had been occurring in Europe at that time – the discovery of the ruins of Pompeii in 1748, the resultant interest and growth of archaeology, and the Grand Tour of Europe. The sons and daughters of the affluent spent months journeying around, seeing first-hand the wonders and mysteries of ancient Greece and Rome, having their portraits painted against backdrops of Classical scenery, and obtaining artefacts for the return home. The ancient world was seen as a model of idealism, purity, nobility and simplicity. The sculpture, which was life-like, realistic and skilfully carved in smooth white marble, was particularly admired. Thus the Neoclassical style was born, in respectful imitation of the original.

Elaborate funerals of the wealthy could be highly expensive. The charges for the funeral of John Bridges (the county historian) at Barton Seagrave in March 1724 came to £146 14s 1d, which included among several items 'an Elme Coffin covered with Lead' (£4), with an inscribed plate (5s), a charge for 'searing' the inside of the Coffin to preserve the body (10s), a superfine shroud sheet cap, pillow and gloves (£1 15s), six men to carry the coffin (9s) and the 'saudering' of the lid before deposition (10s). A wall tablet in the old nave of the church commemorates his death.

By the nineteenth century, however, intramural burials were becoming less commonplace and the more affluent now joined the rest of the community in the churchyard, where their tombs continued to reflect their status, as before. Some had elaborate monuments, such as tall Celtic-style crosses on plinths, life-size angels, or low-pitched versions of the altar tomb, almost at ground level with gables and ridges, coping, or a raised cross on a plinth. Others were given an air of exclusiveness and privacy by being enclosed with iron railings or wide stone kerbing.

DEVELOPMENT OF THE CHURCHYARD

Despite the fashion for the more prosperous to be buried inside the church, there had been early cases where, apart from members of the clergy, certain benefactors preferred a burial in the churchyard along with most of the community, rather than inside. In 1500 John Taylor requested 'to be buried in the churchyard of Our Lady of Blakesley before the crosse in the said churche yarde'. Gregory Boyle of Little Newton (d. 1553) asked 'to be buried in the churchyard of Sent faith at Newton'.

Let us now look at the various types of monument that appeared in the churchyard over time. During the medieval period, an exterior version of the altar tomb became fairly widespread: the chest tomb (alternatively known as the tomb chest). Something like a heightened extension of the earlier lid-covered tomb, and like the altar tomb in shape and purpose, it was hollow and covered the grave beneath the earth. Unlike its internal counterpart, however, the lid did not usually act as a base for an effigy, although some interesting examples of where this did happen have come to light (in all cases they are now housed inside the church), such as that of two slabs of thirteenth-century priests discovered in pristine condition in the tower of the church at Rothwell in 1981. These had the unique feature of drainage holes at the head and feet, which were made to help prevent water from collecting on the carved features. At Little Oakley there is the worn effigy of a thirteenth-century forester, with an arrow under his belt. There is another forester (early fourteenth century) at Glinton, with his horn and a 'shef of pocock awres' (sheaf of peacock feathers) at his side. (The effigy of his wife, however, remains outside.) In the churchyard at Stoke Doyle there is the effigy of a thirteenth-century priest depicted under a trefoiled canopy. It was removed from its original site when the church was rebuilt between 1722 and 1725.

The earliest versions of the chest tomb in the thirteenth century had plain panels at the sides and ends, but in the following century these were engraved with a contemporary tracery design similar to that for windows and fonts. By the fifteenth century they were

A seventeenth-
century chest tomb
in the churchyard
of St James at
Thrapston.

frequently decorated with roundels, cusped quatrefoils and shields, as can be seen at
Corby, Thrapston and Rothwell. Sometimes they were topped with a double-ridged
capstone. In the sixteenth and seventeenth centuries they were usually surmounted by
a flat, thicker and heavier moulded slab/capstone. The side panels in many cases did
not have decorative features, but there was an emphasis on large, deep-set lettering
– the name of the deceased and the date of death. The earliest surviving chest tombs
of this type are at Wadenhoe (1592) and Thrapston (1600). They reached the height
of their popularity during the eighteenth and nineteenth centuries, by which time they
had become plainer with a more solid, classical appearance, both in proportion and
design.

Several have suffered from the ravages of time. The elements, rodents and ivy have
caused the capstone to split or become detached, or the sides to partially cave in. It is
certainly not the result of grave robbers.

However, until 1666, the usual form of churchyard burial for the majority of
people was to be wrapped in a plain linen shroud (winding sheet) tied at both ends
by a designated person who prepared the corpse for the occasion. The poor would
be placed in a common (reusable) coffin, usually made of crude oak, either carried
on the shoulders or transported on the parish bier, which was normally kept at the
rear of the church, many of which can still be seen at places like Benefield, Glapthorn,
Oundle and Nassington. Participants in early funerary processions would usually wear
black, in the form of hoods and cloaks. Rosemary was often thrown onto the coffin
as it was lowered, and graves were usually unmarked. The more prosperous had their
own wooden coffin in which they were buried and in some cases, they did have a
form of a grave marker, initially fashioned from wood and later in stone. It was also
customary upon the death of a farmer to send a wheatsheaf (garb) to his family, partly

as a token of remembrance but also to ensure they would continue to flourish after their supporter had gone, the wheat, like a corn dolly, being a symbol of fertility. The more affluent wore items of jewellery such as mourning rings (from the seventeenth century) and mourning brooches, which became fashionable during the Georgian and Victorian eras, were engraved with the name and date of death of the deceased, and sometimes contained the deceased's image or even a lock of hair.

Funeral expenses for a normal burial in the late eighteenth century were a shadow of what they are today, as can be seen in this 1795 item from Hellidon (jersey was the name for wool, the required material for burial by law at the time). The cost was 17s 7d (87p in today's money):

> Coffin for Widow Clarke, 10/-
> To the clerk for ringing the bell, and the digger of the grave, 1/6d
> To the 4 carriers, 4/-
> For jersey, 7d
> Ale, 6d
> Ann Goodman for laying her out, 1/-

Not all churches had their own burial ground. For example, until 1406, the parishioners of Great Oakley had to carry their dead cross-country and uphill for about two miles, via 'Bier Baulk' (a strip of grassland between fields), to the churchyard of Great Newton.

However, access across land for a funeral procession was not always a straightforward process. Many landowners would expect payment for the privilege. As late as the nineteenth century, such a custom was still fairly widespread, as was the case with Henry Coales, a farmer in Aldwincle parish, who on more than one occasion kept a record/memorandum in his daybook, as seen in the following entry for September 1855:

> Mrs Chapman, Wife of Robert Chapman, who died on the ... Sept 1855, was buried on the 26 Sept 1855, and the Funeral, that is the Corpse, was allowed to be conveyed from Robert Chapman's Lodge through my Farm, on the Gates being unlocked by Thomas, he demanding by my wishes, one Shilling for their being allowed [i.e. the whole funeral] to pass through.

Even where a church did have its own burial site, access was not straightforward, as at Whiston, where, even today, access can only be gained to the churchyard by a field track, due to the high elevation of the church and the lack of a thoroughfare for motor vehicles.

Some churchyards had lychgates at their entrance. They were places to rest the body en route to the grave, and often had gables for shelter. The name derives from an Old Germanic word for a corpse. Most parishes, however, especially the less affluent, did not have one, and instead used a set of flat steps or slabs. Lychgates first appeared after 1549, when the *Book of Common Prayer* required the priest to meet the funeral cortège at the entrance to mark the beginning of the service. They are now rare and those seen in the county today in places such as Islip, Achurch, Benefield, Aldwincle All Saints, Cold Ashby and Silverstone are Victorian in origin.

Stone grave markers became fashionable during the seventeenth century, but the cost was prohibitive for most people, so in virtually every churchyard there are countless unmarked burials lying beneath the surface, a situation compounded by population growth over time, necessitating the creation of more space, either by placing burials on top of existing graves (thereby heightening the ground level) or by extending the churchyard. A look at the number of deaths recorded in parish registers (and, later, the population censuses) for a particular place and a comparison of these with the number of graves – while taking into account members of the community who would have moved elsewhere as a result of marriage, employment and, later, emigration, or removal to a centralised workhouse – shows just how many unmarked graves there are. (Conversely, some churchyard memorials only commemorate a person who has died elsewhere, and so the name does not appear among burials recorded in parish registers.)

In towns like Oundle, where burials became particularly numerous in the nineteenth century, it was necessary to mark each row with a numeral, some of which can still be seen engraved in the wall adjacent to the footpath from New Street. In many places during the same period, an additional stone was often placed at the other end of a grave. These 'footstones' were much smaller than the headstone, and only contained the initials of the deceased and the date of burial. Because they are small, it has mistakenly been assumed that they mark the grave of a child that had predeceased its parents, but this is certainly not so. During maintenance and rearrangement of churchyards in more recent times, some have since been re-sited and placed next to the headstone.

An earlier method of creating more public burial space was to have a charnel house, also known as a bone crypt, bone hole, or ossuary. Remains were dug up in churchyards to create room for fresh burials and the bones of the occupants were deposited in these specially created sites, which lay underground. Only two survive in Britain, one being at Hythe in Kent, where over 2,000 skulls and 8,000 bones are stored. The other is in Northamptonshire, under the south side of the churchyard of Holy Trinity at Rothwell. It was discovered around 1700 by a sexton preparing the ground for a burial. The ground beneath his spade gave way and he found himself in a dark vault, the floor of which was strewn with heaps of bones. It is believed that many of them had been removed to the vault when the south aisle was being extended and the chancel lengthened shortly after 1350. Seventeen steps were subsequently found leading down to the vault, and, on later examination, the east wall was found to have a painted scene in the plaster. Around 1,500 skulls and bones were stored in the crypt, and in 1912 the thigh bones were rearranged into two separate stacks and some of the skulls were displayed on specially made shelving. In life the people had been suffering from common ailments of the time. The bones show signs of rickets, bone outgrowth, fracturing, malignancies, osteoarthritis and other diseases. The inscriptions on headstones of burials in the same churchyard show that the process continued well into later times. The crypt was subsequently opened to the public as an item of curiosity, a practice that continues today at weekends or on special occasions.

Racks of skulls in the bone crypt of the church of Holy Trinity, Rothwell.

In April 1992, a 'secret room' beneath the porch of the church of St Mary and All Saints at Fotheringhay was excavated, three years after its unexpected discovery. There was a blocked-up chute leading from the churchyard that was originally used for depositing piles of bones from the surface when room was being made for new burials. Apart from bones, however, the variety of finds revealed that the chamber had served other purposes: they included broken pots, bottles, stained glass, coins, jettons, tiles, slates, brick, marbles, a penknife and a pair of nutcrackers. It is believed that the room acted as a place for meeting and planning by masons involved in work on the church. Some of the fifteenth-century stained-glass fragments were made into a collage for a window in the east wall of a room (the Upper Room) over the porch in 1994.

In later years, when memorial space was at a premium, or when churchyards were being grassed over, smaller headstones like wall tablets within the church were often set into the boundary walls, as at Benefield and Haselbech; or existing headstones were removed and placed against the walls, as at Corby and Wellingborough; or they were laid flat, as at Towcester.

BURIAL IN WOOLLEN

In 1666, an act was passed ordering that everyone was to be buried in a woollen shroud, in order to stimulate the declining national wool trade with Europe. For years, this had been a highly profitable venture with European neighbours, who had great regard for the quality of the product.

However, non-compliance led to a second act coming into force in 1678, to ensure the custom was carried out to the satisfaction of the law. An affidavit had to be issued within eight days of interment. This did not go down well with many priests, who had to ensure that the affidavit had been produced by those concerned, an oath made in their presence, and any necessary paperwork or records completed, thereby placing an additional burden on their everyday duties. This showed in some of the priests' comments – some sardonic, some tinged with sarcasm, some over-meticulous and long-winded. A typical reaction was that of the priest at Helmdon, who in the 1680s continually made his feelings known, one example being in June 1680:

> Thomas Shortland, son of Thomas Shortland, being Dead, was put into a Pit-hole and Bury'd in the churchyard of the Town above written … [and] was well wrapt in a shirt of Woollen, and was let down into his Dormitory with that vestment about his corps to the great satisfaction of the Law, enjoining that Habilment as convenient for the Dead.

There could also be a touch of humour in these entries, such as that recorded in 1682, also at Helmdon: 'Frances Pickering was shrowded only in a winding sheet made of the Fleece of good Fat Mutton.' Some of the more compliant clergy also recorded burials in the parish register in unique ways, as was the case at Clipston in the eighteenth century where at one stage an 'X' was marked next to the name of the deceased.

A typical Northamptonshire 'burial in woollen' certificate.

Many wealthy parishioners also objected to the new order and broke the law, preferring to be buried according to their own wishes. Up to £5 could be the penalty, which would be paid by representatives of the deceased. Half of this would go to the informant of the offence, and half to the poor. For example, in May 1731:

> Mary Palmer, Widdow, was Buried in Linnen. The Penalty was paid by the Executors and distributed as the Law in that case directs.

Even where burials in woollen were just about affordable, marking the grave with a headstone was not. At Great Oakley in 1686, there were eleven burials in woollen recorded in the parish register, yet today there are only two (adjacent) headstones in the well-preserved churchyard, where apart from some fallen and damaged headstones, things otherwise seem to have remained intact.

The custom of burial in woollen was to last for nearly 150 years; it was finally abolished in 1814.

NOTABLE MONUMENTS

During the nineteenth century, some churchyard monuments became elaborate like their internal counterparts, a few of which invite comment because of their uniqueness in appearance. At the south-east corner of the churchyard at Middleton Cheney stands a fine Victorian Gothic Revival 'sepulchre' designed by the Oxford-based architect William Wilkinson (1819–1901) and carved by Thomas Earp (1828–83), who is famed for making the replacement Eleanor Cross at Charing Cross in London. The sepulchre is a memorial to the Horton family and dates from 1867. It is a multiple-arched structure of limestone and marble, with ornate finials and a roof with slates laid in a fish scale-like pattern. The Horton family were lords of the manor who had made their fortune with textile machinery at the end of the eighteenth century. At Hellidon, there is the 'Holthouse Cross', a memorial to Charles S. Holthouse, who was vicar from 1845 to 1888. It was designed by the nationally renowned architect William Butterfield in the form of a foliated cross with a tapering shaft on a sloping-sided rectangular base, on which there is an inscription framed by foiled arches.

At Haselbech, a number of grave markers stand out as being different from the normal type of funerary monument found in English churchyards. Two of these, on the north-west side, are solid, horizontal sarcophagi to Charles and Mathilda Bower (who died in 1924 and 1963, respectively). He was the third son of the American shipping magnate Thomas Ismay, who owned the White Star Shipping Company (which later became part of Cunard). It was Charles's brother, the future owner of the company, who named the *Titanic*. Charles lived at Haselbech Hall with his wife and two sons, who later acquired British citizenship. A racehorse owner and passionate hunter, riding with the Pytchley Hunt, he also liked indulging in big-game hunting in Africa, hence the frieze on his tomb with elaborate carvings of animals. The same uniqueness can be applied to another memorial to him, also from 1924, in the south aisle of the

The ornate Victorian Gothic tomb of the Horton family in the churchyard of All Saints, Middleton Cheney.

church itself: a wall tablet with a painted image of St George, commissioned by his brothers and sisters. Close by is another fascinating monument: that of Elizabeth Pell (*d.* 1907) and her husband, Albert (1825–94), who lived at Haselbech Hill. She was churchwarden and a great nature lover, 'the tender protector of God's creatures', hence the incorporation of a large spider's web in the design of the ironwork for the memorial. Their actual burial spot is in the churchyard, close to the porch.

SUICIDES AND 'UNNATURAL' DEATHS AND BURIALS

The worst form of death in the eyes of our ancestors was the unnatural kind: suicide, or 'felo de se' (literally 'a felon of oneself'). It was considered a mortal sin, one greater than fornication or adultery, and dying unrepentant without absolution from one's sins was spiritual anathema. It was widely believed that the Devil was anxious to secure the bodies of the wicked so that he could subject them to extreme forms of torture. Since the burial of suicides in consecrated ground was against common law, and prohibited by civil law until the second quarter of the nineteenth century, burials were made at an alternative, more unobtrusive place to make it more difficult for the Devil to achieve

LINES

OCCASIONED BY THE

DEATH OF WILLIAM MURDIN

OF LITTLE OAKLEY,

WHO WAS FOUND DROWNED IN A POND IN HIS CLOSE,

On the 21st of December, 1847.

Poor Murdin could not rest
During the shortest day :
His mind was quite distres'd,
And so he went away

From family and home,
And went up to his close
To seek a wat'ry tomb ;
As we may now suppose.

'Twas in the afternoon,
He said he'd take a walk ;
His wife expected soon
He would be coming back.

Some bushes in his field
A deepish pond surround :
He there to death did yield ;
He in that pond was drown'd.

So he came back no more
Possessed of life and breath ;
But was brought to his door
A specimen of death !

The corpse was homeward borne
At ten o'clock at night.
To see his kindred mourn,
Was an affecting sight.

His children lov'd him much
While he was living here ;
The loss to them is such
As no man can repair.

O might the fatherless
In Jesus find a friend :
May He the widow bless,
And always her defend.

And let it now be known,
That God preserves our breath,
For we do every one
Deserve Eternal death.

For sinners Jesus died ;
But by the Holy Ghost
We must be sanctified,
Or we shall all be lost.

David Townsend.

Geddington, Dec. 22, 1847.

A broadsheet ballad by blacksmith David Townsend, recording the death of William Murdin at Little Oakley.

his aims, usually beside the highway, or better still at a crossroads (whose shape was symbolic). Often the body would be pinned down with a heavy object, or even staked.

However, there was a tendency, when an 1823 act came into force forbidding burials at crossroads, to allow a normal interment in the churchyard or cemetery, but only late at night. Such was the case of a twenty-three-year-old gamekeeper at Sibbertoft, who was placed in an unmarked grave (only recently located) to the north of the church. On Boxing Day 1848, a Northampton man fatally stabbed a woman to death, after which he drowned himself in the Nene; he was subsequently buried as a suicide at midnight in the churchyard of St Giles. Another suicide took place on Midwinter Day in 1847. William Murdin, a farmer who lived in Little Oakley where his wife, Anne, ran the village alehouse, the Duke's Arms, went for a late afternoon walk, and headed off in the direction of his fields, his mind in some kind of turmoil. As he had not returned by nightfall, a search was made by the villagers that ultimately led to the tragic discovery of Oakley's body in a pond. At the inquest, the verdict was given as suicide, not accidental death. The reasons for his suicide have never been satisfactorily explained, but the following day, his good friend, the former village blacksmith, musician and poet, David Townsend – who had moved to nearby Geddington to set up a forge some time earlier – wrote a ballad to memorialise the event.

In the previous century, however, the bodies of some suicides were not allowed to be at rest. One such example was recorded in the parish registers for Overstone in December 1719. When Rebecca Adams was buried that month, the vicar stated that her husband had cut his throat the previous year and had been buried at the corner of a hedge 'by ye Northfield closes', only to be secretly removed on two occasions, 'in order to be made a skeleton' for a Northampton surgeon named Stephenson.

EXCOMMUNICATION

The act of excommunication – official exclusion of a person from membership of the Church – was due to a lack of conformity, a moral offence, or a failure to meet one's traditional obligations (i.e. non-payment of either Easter dues or tithes, something not popular after the Reformation, and which ultimately disappeared with the Tithe Commutation Act of 1831, which saw the traditional custom replaced by rents). Originally, excommunication was carried out via the 'bell, book and candle' ceremony in which a Bible was closed, a candle quenched, and a bell tolled – as if a death had occurred. Preston Capes seems to have had the highest number of excommunications in the county, with fourteen being carried out over a twenty-six-year period beginning in 1617. Eventual absolution was possible, but for the duration of excommunication, the right to burial on hallowed ground was prohibited. There are often references to this, as was the case at Islip:

> Oct 30th, 1771, Henry Baker, farmer, died before the sentence of excommunication was taken off. Consequently he was refused a Christian burial.

However, burials were sometimes carried out in secret, such as at Weedon Bec in 1615, but there could be consequences:

> William Radhouse, the elder, dying excommunicate, was buried by stealth in the night time in the churchyard 29 January. Wherefore the church was interdicted for a fortnight.

BAPTISM AND CHRISOM BURIALS

Due to the relative transience of life and the vulnerability of the baby's soul in the face of spiritual attack by evil forces, it was considered vital to baptise the baby as quickly as possible after birth. It was believed in some places that an unbaptised child would be attacked, deprived of its life and carried off to the infernal regions, and as late as the nineteenth century it was commonly thought that if a child died unbaptised and without a name, its spirit would wander restlessly around the neighbourhood, unable to rest. Therefore, the first day of the baby's life was the preferred time for the ceremony to take place. Following the anointing with specially consecrated chrisom oil (usually a mixture of olive oil and balsam), the heads of babies were covered with a linen kerchief known as the 'chrisom cloth' (similar to the 'care cloth' that was once placed over the heads of a newly married couple after receiving the blessing at their wedding). The cloth was then wrapped around the body of the baby, and if death occurred within a month, it acted as a shroud for the burial. This was all too common an occurrence, as can be seen in parish registers such as this entry for Nassington, 1623/24:

> A crisum childe of John Bandons bur[ie]d March, it departed presently after it was borne.

However, this was not always a straightforward practice. During the nineteenth century, a vicar of Sibbertoft upset the village by refusing to have a chrisom child buried in the churchyard. The incensed women of the village took matters into their own hands by diverting the constable's attention elsewhere, whereupon they locked the vicar inside the church as a punishment.

Another practice sometimes carried out when a child died early, whether baptised or not, was to bury it under the eaves of the church, so that the rainwater pouring off the roof would provide constant baptism.

HEART BURIALS

It was sometimes customary during the medieval period for those of wealth or position who had died far from home to have two burials. The body, with the heart removed, would be interred at the place of death. The heart was then was embalmed in some form and sent back to the original domicile, or another place once associated with the deceased. The earliest known case in Northamptonshire was that of Robert de Mellent, Earl of Leicester, who died in Paris in 1118. He had earlier founded the Hospital of St John and St James in Brackley, and it was to here that his heart was brought from France in a salt-filled lead casket and buried in the hospital chapel (now demolished).

The same hospital was the site of a similar burial in 1235, when Margaret, Countess of Winchester, died. A shrine was erected there as a depository for her heart. Years later, her son ordered a measure of corn to be fashioned into the shape of a coffin and placed on display next to the heart. He further instructed that this receptacle should be filled three times a year with corn from his land at Woodford Halse, for the use of the hospital inmates.

Highly visible today is the heart uncovered by workmen restoring the north aisle of the church of St Mary at Woodford during the spring of 1866. While removing a beam from a transitional arch, they came across some broken fragments of masonry concealing a stone recess, within which was deposited a bamboo box wrapped in coarse cloth. On opening the box, they were astonished to find an embalmed heart, which was later deemed most likely to be that of Sir Roger de Kirketon, who had died in Norfolk, where he was buried in 1280 – minus his heart. The organ was subsequently brought to Woodford, the original home of his wife. On the completion of repairs, the heart was placed in a pillar in the south aisle, in a freshly prepared recess with a glass panel for viewing.

Another heart is said to have been entombed at the church of St Mary at Great Brington. It is supposedly that of twenty-three-year-old Henry Spencer, who was killed by a cannonball at the Battle of Naseby while attending Charles I. A leaden container in the church – without an inscription or a date and apparently never opened – is said to hold his heart.

A reverse situation occurred in the nineteenth century – one of national significance, but also one with a notable Northamptonshire connection. The rector of Twywell, the Revd Horace Waller, was a great friend of Dr David Livingstone, the renowned Scottish missionary and explorer. Searching for the sources of the rivers Nile, Zambezi and Congo, he discovered the Victoria Falls on the great Zambezi. Apart from establishing missionary centres, Livingstone campaigned against the slave trade and helped to open up the commercial routes that led to improved economic prosperity in the region. When he died on 1 May 1873, his two devoted servants, Susi and Chuma, decided that the body should be returned to Britain.

They buried his heart under a tree and, after embalming the body, wrapped it in a covering of bark and carried it on foot through hazardous countryside, which was infested with crocodiles, pythons and other dangerous animals. They crossed a 4-mile wide river to reach the coast, which lay 800 miles away. At one stage they had to disguise their burden as a bale of cotton in order to pass safely through the territory of a warlike tribal chieftain. Having safely negotiated this, they accompanied the body by steamship, and finally reached England, where the body was buried in Westminster Abbey in April 1874. The bark that they had used for transporting the body was brought to Twywell, where the Revd Horace Waller received them. They helped Waller to research his friend's life and edit his journals. Fragments of the bark can be seen in the vestry of the church today.

EXECUTIONS

Most crimes in England were considered to be a felony, i.e. a civil crime, including murder, theft, robbery and forgery. Felonies were usually punished by hanging (and later by transportation or hard labour), regardless of age or gender. For example, in 1750 a seventeen-year-old boy was hanged as an accomplice to highway robbery. Four years later, another boy, William Love, was hanged for stealing money from a house at Wellingborough.

After hanging, the worst criminals were placed on a gibbet and their remains were left to crows and to the elements, one noteworthy case being that of Bryan Connell, whose crime was so hideous that it received national coverage. In 1739 he had been involved in the murder of Richard Brimley, a butcher in Weedon Lois. The press reported, 'He gave him fourteen or fifteen wounds and cut off his Head so that it hung only by its Sinews.' His subsequent execution in April 1741, two years after he was finally caught, was witnessed by a huge gathering at Northampton Heath (now Northampton Racecourse), the site of the county gallows. It was further reported:

> To the last the culprit strenuously denied his guilt. After the execution, the body, pursuant to the sentence, was removed to Weedon Common, near the scene of the tragedy, and there it was hung in chains on a gibbet, within sight of the door of his

mother's house. For months the rotting corpse swayed in the wind, and the rattle of the chains was supposed to be a constant, ever present warning to the evil.

The gibbet also featured after an execution at Northampton in March 1738, when John Cotton, who had murdered his child, was hanged on the gallows for 'about an hour'. The body was then placed 'in irons with rivets around it forming a kind of cage' and carried to the common at Paulerspury, where it was hung 'as a terror to the countryside'.

Penalties for such crimes were compounded further after an act passed in 1752 ordained that, following sentence, the guilty were to be given a diet of bread and water for thirty-six hours, and that after hanging, the body was to either be hung in chains or 'given to the surgeons to be anatomized' (i.e. dissected). One of the first convicted people in the county to undergo this punishment was a young single woman, Ann Loale, who was found guilty of murdering a child in March 1759. She died insisting that it had been her master who had carried out the deed.

A perhaps more barbarous form of death sentence was carried out in 1630 at Northampton's New Pasture (site of the later Spencer Parade), when a criminal was 'pressed to death'. This was a protracted process, spread out over a few days, during which the person was 'laid on his back on the bare floor, naked, unless where decency forbade', whereupon a heavy iron weight was placed on his body 'as he could bear and more'. Thereafter, he could have no sustenance except for three morsels of 'the worst brede', and, on the second day, three draughts of 'standing water' placed near the prison door. The process was repeated until death ended the criminal's misery.

In England the crime of witchcraft had also been a felony (punishable by hanging), unlike in Scotland and Europe, where it was a heresy (i.e. a crime against the Church) and therefore punishable by burning. However, in one case burning took place *after* the hanging of two convicted women, Elinor Shaw and Mary Philips, on the gallows at Abington in March 1705. It was ordered that they were 'to be hanged till they are almost Dead and then surrounded with Faggots, Pitch and other Combustible matter, which being set on Fire, their bodies are to be consumed to Ashes'. This superstitious practice – to ensure that such crimes would not be committed again, or that revenge would not be taken by the deceased – was not completely rare, and was in some ways a throwback to prehistoric times. One notable example occurred in Essex in the seventeenth century, when a large rock was used to weigh down the body of a freshly hanged 'witch'.

There were several burnings in the county for another crime, however – that of petty treason (the attempted overthrow of an authority), such as the poisoning of a husband by a wife (but not the other way around). This may seem strange to us today, but it was a form of treason until as late as 1828, when it was finally abolished. One of the earliest recorded burnings for the offence was that of 'Mrs Lucas' of Moulton in 1631, followed in 1645 by another female burning between 'the river and Delapré Abbey', and another ten years later at Boughton Green. In 1715 Elizabeth Trasler of Badby was burnt at Northampton Heath, and yet another burning took place there in 1735 – that of Elizabeth Fawson, the last woman in the county to be burnt for such a crime

The mutilated inscription on the effigy of Mabila de Murdak at Gayton.

(although another woman, May Hadon, also met the same fate the following year – for murdering her mother). In many cases, the 'victim' would be strangled by the executioner to render the body insensible before it was consigned to the flames. This was the case with Elizabeth Fawson, as was recorded in a broadsheet printed by the *Northampton Mercury*, in which she was described as being dragged on a sledge (not a cart, as was usual) to the execution site, where, as requested, a private attendant was present to make sure she was 'quite dead for some time' – a rope was placed around her neck before she was tied to the stake and the fire lit. The broadsheet added that 'in about two or three hours she was entirely consumed'.

Interestingly, at Weedon Lois there is a badly eroded eighteenth-century headstone in the churchyard of St Mary, supposedly depicting a female figure handing a man a poisoned drink. According to an unsubstantiated tradition, *this* was the last woman in the county ever to be burnt for such a crime (although there is no record of this person in the parish registers, which date from as far back as 1559). It seems strange that an allusion to such a heretical deed would ever be depicted on a memorial, and that the person even received such a burial marker at all.

An interesting comparison with this can be made with a more remarkable visual testament to the crime of murdering a husband. When workmen were restoring part of the chancel in the church of St Mary at Gayton in 1830, they came across a small stone effigy of Mabila de Murdak concealed in the walling. Close by today are the effigies of a former lord of the manor, Sir Philip de Gayton (*d.* 1316), and one of his daughters, Scholastica/Escholace (*d.* 1345). Another daughter, Juliana, married Thomas de Murdak of Edgcote, whom she later poisoned. Consequently, she paid the ultimate penalty for such a deed at the stake in 1310. It was her daughter's effigy that the workmen discovered. It had most likely been hidden because of her mother's crime. However, more revealing is the fact that part of the inscription – that of her surname – was gouged out at some point, perhaps as a sign of contempt and shame. The effigy can be seen today in a recess, together with that of Aunt Scholastica.

Although technically not an execution, a death sentence was pronounced on a pro-Royalist vicar of Wellingborough, Mr Jones, for constantly preaching against the Parliamentarian government of the 1650s. On the second occasion that he was dragged out of church by an angry mob, he was taken to Northampton, where he was locked up and starved to death. The mayor of Northampton then ordered that when the bones of 'the starved martyr' were buried, the only epitaph should be, 'Ashes to ashes,/Dust to dust,/Here's the Pit,/And in you must!'

CATHOLICS AND NONCONFORMISTS

Inevitably, there was stubborn resistance among recusants – usually the wealthier elements of society – who illegally adhered to the old Catholic faith instead of the state religion (established by the Act of Supremacy in 1534) and paid the penalty with heavy fines and/or imprisonment for non-attendance of church, concealing a Jesuit priest, saying Mass, etc. They included a number of priests. For example, in 1581 Thomas Fletcher, the vicar of Scaldwell, stipulated in his will that he wanted 'a *Catholic* burial', with the best vestments draped over his corpse and the parish chalice held upright on his breast by having his stole (a strip of silk) pinned across it.

During the brief relapse into Catholicism under Queen Mary between 1553 and 1558, there were repercussions for anyone wavering from the re-established faith. One significant victim was a poor, illiterate shoemaker from Syresham, John Kurde. It is believed that a local cleric with a grudge managed to get him arrested for denying 'Popish doctrine'. He was consequently taken to Northampton, and after interrogation was sentenced to a fiery death as a heretic. As he stood at the stake by the town gates, a Catholic priest stood by, promising a pardon if he recanted, to which Kurde is supposed to have replied, '*Christ* gave his pardon.' In the Wesleyan chapel at his home village of Syresham, a brass plate was later mounted on the wall, inscribed 'burnt at the stake in defence of the truth'.

The situation would be further exacerbated during the following century, with Nonconformists such as Baptists, Presbyterians and Quakers, and the ejection of Puritan incumbents (one in five nationally by 1662, and a total of sixty in Northamptonshire, fourteen of whom later recanted). One of the more prominent ejected ministers was Thomas Maydwell, a native of Geddington, who had been rector of Kettering for twelve years and who went on to become one of the most highly regarded Nonconformists of that era. He was, however, buried in the chancel of his former church in January 1692, with a ledger inscribed in Latin (it is barely legible today).

One of the earliest Nonconformists was 'the Father of Puritanism', Robert Browne (born *c.* 1550), whose family were prominent merchants in Northamptonshire. Constantly in trouble with Church authorities, imprisoned and exiled for preaching that

God was the only real authority, he soon attracted hordes of followers, the Brownists. After being threatened with excommunication in 1586, however, he recanted and became the rector of Achurch. He died in Northampton in 1633, and he is buried in the churchyard of St Giles. A memorial marks his resting place.

The county had two early Baptist churches during the Commonwealth (1649–60), at Ravensthorpe and Peterborough. By the 1700s the Baptists had become widely established. One of their finest chapels is at Clipston. It was built in 1803 by the renowned county architect Edmund Law of Northampton; the ornate front was added in 1864. The churchyard is relatively large and contains the tomb of a noted hymn writer, Thomas Jarman (to whom there is also a plaque at the entrance to the church).

Religious meetings of over five people were banned, with the Quakers in particular being hard-hit: between 1654 and 1686, more than 490 of them were imprisoned in the county. Fourteen died during that period, and fifteen were banished to Jamaica. Finedon and Bugbrooke in particular suffered heavily from persecution. In Northampton, several men, women, children and 'suckling babies' were sent to prison on 7 March 1685 for attending meetings, 'absence from church' and not complying with other statutory obligations. Thomas Boone of Corby was fined for being present at the interment of his own wife on 21 April 1686 'as a transgressor of the law against conventicles [secret meetings]' and 'suffered Distress of his Goods for that supposed offence, to the value 7 shillings'.

The Act of Toleration in 1688 finally allowed Nonconformists to attend their own religious meetings, although there were still some restrictions, and fines continued to be imposed for the non-payment of tithes. Quaker burials did not take place in Anglican churchyards, but parish priests were often informed of such an occasion:

- 'Thomas Seamark informed me yt [that] one William Faukner was buried in an orchard belonging to Emanuel Boone on ye 17th of October, 1703.' (Corby)
- John Green buried his wife by his orchard wall. (Clipston, 1751. The parish register also recorded John Green's burial in the same orchard eight years later.)

Quaker minute books give details of similar burials, such as those of Mary White of Corby, who 'was buried in her own garden' on 29 August 1743, and Frances Cook of Weldon, who was 'buried in his own place' on 22 June 1750.

Although Nonconformists saw burial in consecrated ground as meaningless (a field or garden being just as suitable or sacrosanct, like modern eco-burials), in many cases they *were* buried in parish churchyards until they had their own burial grounds. At Geddington, the Quaker burial ground was at the rear of the cottage (built *c.* 1729) where they met, and interments continued to be made there until the 1870s. The gravestones subsequently disappeared, and according to local rumour they were used to build an inner partition during later renovations. In the 1950s a builder uncovered eighteen skeletons and, with due consideration, they were reburied on the other side of the garden wall, as close as possible to the original site. At Duddington, a meeting house and burial ground was established in the main street; it was sold at the beginning of the nineteenth century.

There could be a certain amount of unjustified hostility and antagonism towards Nonconformists. An early example of this appeared in the parish registers of Bugbrooke in 1662:

> Margaret Goodwin, widow, was buried May 5th 1662, the minister, Mr John Whitfield, was thrown into the grave by a cruell and curst sort of people called Quakers, not without danger of being there buried alive, which he has left upon record to live when he is dead.

The Independent Chapel at Rothwell is one of the earliest Congregationalist churches in England. Meetings were held in a barn from 1655 until the church was built in 1735. It soon attracted worshippers from a wide area (from as far away as Northampton, Wellingborough and Hallaton in Leicestershire). They would make their way across fields on foot with lanterns, or on horseback. Initially, burials were in the parish churchyard, where the first three pastors were interred. The first one, John Beverley, died in 1658 and stipulated that his grave was to be unmarked. The second pastor, John Browning, was buried in 1685, north-east of the chancel. The inscription on his tomb was recut in the 1860s, and while workmen were restoring the stonework, a group of inmates from the adjacent Jesus Hospital gathered around to try to decipher the Latin inscription. Their attempts at interpreting individual words with no knowledge of Latin are somewhat amusing: one man saw the word 'eccliae' and believed it meant that the pastor used to preach out of the Book of Ecclesiastes; another thought that the phrase 'Conveniebat pastor' alluded to Browning being ever-ready to supply the needs of any chapel; others felt that 'publice' meant the priest had once been a publican. Perhaps the most amusing interpretation of all, however, was that of one man who thought that 'fungendo opera' meant that the pastor had been some kind of opera singer.

The next three pastors were buried close to the pulpit in their chapel, the ledger of a later pastor, Richard Davis (1714), reading, 'Here lyes meanest Dust,/Whom God of his own good pleasure,/Out of his rich glorious Treasure,/Of grace did ere entrust.'

Land was finally purchased for a Congregationalist burial ground in 1839, and the first interment was that of Elizabeth Oran in March 1840, the headstone having an added inscription: 'This was the first corpse interred in the burial ground. My flesh shall rest in the ground,/Till the last trumpet's joyful sound,/Then with faith I will arise,/With them to reign above the skies.'

Ashley had another Congregationalist chapel (1673) that attracted worshippers from far and wide, in this case from thirteen villages, but they suffered persecution by the local rector, who on one occasion, in 1717, persuaded the local militia to set fire to the premises (they failed). Subsequently, some of the congregation carried firearms to protect the chapel. Land for burials was purchased in 1831, and a few headstones still survive at the rear of the building, overlooking a field and the road to Stoke Albany.

In 1676, Wellingborough had 193 Congregationalists (based in Cheese Lane, and later Silver Street), but in 1812 a breakaway group led by Adam Corrie established its own chapel in what is now Salem Lane. The small forecourt is now a parking area, containing flat gravestones of some of the congregation.

ROMANY BURIALS

Despite their nomadic existence and their belief in the transmutaton of souls, it is known that for centuries Romany gypsies considered burial in a Christian churchyard of importance, but carried out the ceremony in their own special way. When a death occurred, it was customary for the body to be taken outside the caravan, away from the living. The Romany were particularly choosy about where they were buried, preferring a more secluded or elevated churchyard such as those at Pytchley and Gretton, sometimes travelling great distances from the scene of a death to reach one of their favourite burial sites. Graves were not marked with any kind of memorial and the deceased was buried with a valued possession or a lucky amulet for the journey to the afterlife. A number of gypsies eventually settled down at a favourite site, integrated with the inhabitants and contributed their skills, as was the case at Kingscliffe. One such person was Reservoir Woods of Gretton, who acted as wise woman and midwife to rich and poor alike, using her knowledge of plants and herbs for easing all kinds of ailments. On her death in 1911, an elaborate marble headstone was erected by the grateful community; it is prominent in the churchyard today.

MASS BURIALS

The circumstances of mass burials mean they tend to go unrecorded, an example being the immense slaughter that took place in a field which 'lay between Hardingstone and Delapré Abbey' during the Wars of the Roses in July 1460, when the Yorkist faction gained a significant victory over the Lancastrians. King Henry VI was taken prisoner and around 500 men were slain – the battleground was described as looking 'like a sea of blood'. Another battle that took place in the county during the same war was the Battle of Danesmoor at Edgcote in 1469. In this instance, however, rows of pits filled with bones and a quantity of spurs were discovered at neighbouring Chipping Warden during the nineteenth century.

A similar situation to that which had taken place near Hardingstone occurred in the aftermath of the 'Newton Rebellion' in June 1607 at the Brand, near Little Oakley, where a large group of peasants from the region began tearing up hedges and fences that had been illegally put up by Thomas Tresham, depriving local villages of their common rights – a process happening around the Midlands at the time. In the ensuing confrontation with the militia, at least fifty rebels were killed. Strangely, no burials from this event are recorded in the surviving parish registers of local churches.

Of greater renown was the English Civil War of 1642–51. The registers for Middleton Cheney record the interment of forty-six Parliamentarian soldiers in the churchyard in May 1643. This was only a fraction of the 220 or so men killed the day before in the 'Town Field'. Not recorded, however, was where the bodies of well over a hundred Parliamentarian troops were buried after they were attacked by Royalists as they made their way from Weedon Bec towards Borough Hill in February 1645.

After the Battle of Naseby in June 1645, hundreds of slain troops lay in unmarked graves in the vicinity, one survivor recalling, 'I saw the field so bestrewed with Carcasses of Horse and Men as was most sad to behold.' Strangely, however, nothing about the battle was recorded in the parish registers of the village church of All Saints. Various traditions subsequently sprang up, with unverified claims that bodies were disposed of in mass graves in a field west of Sulby, and in the churchyards of Marston Trussell (in the 'Cavaliers' Grave', where Royalists were penned in and slaughtered by pursuing Parliamentarian troops), Harrington, Rushton, and Rothwell. Nothing in the registers of the respective churches is forthcoming. What is known, however, is that over 4,000 Royalist prisoners were taken to Northampton. Many of those who were mortally wounded were subsequently buried in the churchyards of All Saints, St Giles and Holy Sepulchre, and elsewhere in the town.

MAIDENS' GARLANDS

If a young girl died unmarried, a special funerary ceremony was often performed, which was a way of honouring her chastity (a reflection of the way virgin saints like St Agnes, St Barbara and especially St Catherine – 'the Bride of Christ' – were venerated before the Reformation). There were variations in the way the custom was conducted (like the annual May ceremony), but the basic idea was to design and make a small garland, crown, bell or garment of withies, flowers, foliage or other material, and carry it on a pole (often borne by a girl or girls of approximately the same age as the deceased) to accompany the body in procession to the church, where it would be placed in a particular area of the church, such as on a wall above or beneath the place where the girl regularly sat during a service. The custom reached its peak in the latter part of the eighteenth century, after which it slowly died out, like many other customs in the years that followed.

These temporary memorials would often be removed after a set period of mourning and burnt or buried at the graveside. In other cases, they would remain in the church, where, due to the transience of the material, or during a process of restoration or clearance within the church, all traces would vanish. However, two 'survivors' of this custom were recorded in the county in the mid-1800s. One was at Little Harrowden, and was in the form of hoops decorated with white rosettes and suspended from one of the nave arches, where it stayed for many years afterwards. The other was at Maxey, and consisted of a wooden hoop with two black, white and coloured bands crossing each other at right angles above it, forming a kind of crown. The ribs were adorned with paper flowers and other forms of ornamentation. It was placed on the sill of the south-east window in the nave.

We can get a better insight into the custom in the work of one particularly celebrated Northamptonshire clergyman thanks to his highly influential and nationally acclaimed three-volume collection of ballads, *Reliques of Ancient English Poetry*, published in 1765. Thomas Percy came to the county in 1753, at the age of twenty-four, and for twenty-nine years he was vicar at the church of St Peter and St Paul at Easton Maudit.

During this time, he became associated with the church of St Mary at Wilby. He married a girl from Desborough (to whom he proposed in verse) and settled down to a busy life, writing a number of books. With a great antiquarian interest in customs, old ballads and legends (the Holy Grail is supposed to have appeared during his incumbency at Easton Maudit), and influenced by his friend the author Dr Samuel Johnson, he searched around for more material to add to his collection, the result of which was the publication of *Reliques*. In two of the poems in the third volume, Percy refers to the custom of garlands. The first is 'Corydon's Doleful Knell', a poem set in the time of Elizabeth I about a shepherd who loses his sweetheart before their wedding:

> Her corpse shall be attended,
> By maides in fair array,
> Till the obsequities are ended,
> And she is in the clay.
>
> A garland shall be framed,
> By art and nature's skill,
> Of sundry colour'd flowers,
> In token of good will.

The second is 'The Bride's Burial', in which a newly wedded girl dies before the consummation of her marriage. In this variation of the custom, the garland is buried with her:

> A garland fresh and faire,
> Of lilies there was made,
> In sign of her virginitye,
> And on her coffin laid.
>
> Six maidens all in white,
> Did beare her to the ground,
> The bells did ring in solemn sort,
> And made a doleful sound.

THE STRANGE, THE MYSTERIOUS AND THE REMARKABLE

Langton Freeman was born in Whilton and became lord of the manor upon the death of his father. He did not marry and became a clergyman, serving first at Hellidon in 1735, then at Long Buckby, where he became vicar for a period of time, before moving to Warwickshire. Upon his retirement, he returned to the family seat, where he died in 1783. Strangely, there is no record of his burial in the parish registers. In his will he had made generous provision for all four villages with which he had been associated by leaving monetary gifts. But there was also one astonishing clause regarding his burial – a strange list of conditions.

He ordered that his body was to lie on a feather bed for four days until it was 'offensive' (this was not done); then it was to be wrapped in a strong double winding sheet, and carried out to the summer house, which was built onto the south wall of the garden, and in which he was to be placed inside; the doors and windows were to be painted blue, and then locked and bolted 'for ever'; it was to be fenced off with iron or wooden pales, and evergreens were to be planted everywhere in the garden. As the years rolled by, the building became ruinous and covered in ivy, with the roof and a wall collapsing. The body was exposed in a mummified state with no wrappings, 'with one arm lying down by the side, the other across its chest'.

The Revd Francis Tolson, rector of Easton Maudit in 1732–45, was for some unexplained reason not buried in wool as custom dictated at the time. As a result, to the consternation of the villagers, it was said that he was unable to rest and was seen making a nightly walk from his grave to the vicarage pond. Thereafter a ritual known as 'the national laying of ghosts' was arranged during the eighteenth and nineteenth centuries, in which twelve clergymen carried thirteen candles to the 'haunted' site, where the distraught spirit was said to try to extinguish the flames and fierce, and unbridled Bible reading would take place ('reading down the ghost'). This took a lot of resolve and only the strongest-willed participants were chosen for the task. At Easton Maudit they completed the ceremony by throwing their candles into the pond, after which time the perturbed spirit troubled the community no more.

At Deene, Lady Adeline, wife of the 5th Earl of Cardigan, commissioned a specially made coffin long before her death in 1915, at the age of ninety-one. It was kept on a trestle table in the ballroom, where she invited her guests to climb in and give their opinions about its size and comfort.

Another 'advance' burial arrangement occurred at the church of the Holy Cross in Milton Malsor, during the incumbency of George Oakes Miller (1799–1823), who was having his grave plot dug within the chancel. While the work was in progress, he felt that the space was too small, and argued the point with the sexton, who begged to differ. He then climbed into the space and found that the sexton had been right all along.

Devotion to horses and a love of riding have resulted in some unusual burial requests. There have been cases around Britain where the deceased has been buried in full hunting or riding regalia, sometimes standing in an upright position, as was rumoured to have once happened at Haselbech, according to family tradition. At Deene Park, the 5th Earl of Cardigan wanted some form of permanent memorial to his favourite horse, Ronald, which he had ridden during the Crimean War, notably in the Charge of the Light Brigade at Balaclava in October 1854. When the horse died, he had the head embalmed and displayed on the wall of one of the rooms of the great house, where it can be seen today. At nearby Laxton in 1910, a former high sheriff of the county directed that Tommy, his old shooting pony, should be shot within fourteen days of his demise, and buried with its skin on unless his son 'should desire the skin for personal use'.

In May 1907, a former horseman in the 2nd Dragoon Guards who had died at Eastcote Hall, Pattishall, stipulated in his will that he wished to be buried in the gorse bushes at Eastcote with no clergyman in attendance, and that 'my bay mare is to be buried with me, otherwise my bay mare, Dolly Varden, is to be shot, and buried in the paddock at Eastcote, but her tail and one of her feet are to be put in my coffin, as also one of Nancy Lee's feet'. He added that if his wishes could not be carried out, he desired burial in the churchyard at Hartwell.

More malicious perhaps was the behaviour of one Lady Villiers of Sulby Hall. While passing through the village of Sibbertoft on her way to church one Sunday morning in 1890, Lady Villiers became furious when, on the Day of Rest, she saw laundry hanging up to dry outside the cottage of a family in her service. She subsequently dismissed them from her employment. Later, in the terms in her will of 1897 regarding her funeral, she stipulated that two black horses were to pull her cortège – and that they were to be shot afterwards. She is also said to have insisted on wearing her jewellery when buried.

In April 1743, a 'beggar's funeral' took place at the church of All Saints in Northampton. It was for Anne Johnson, a well-known vagrant frequently seen begging for alms around the streets of the town. What is remarkable about the burial was that it took place 'in a handsome manner'. It was subsequently found that such an opulent occasion was part-financed from the vast sum of £400 she had accumulated from her begging activities throughout the years.

In 1790, during groundwork maintenance and the resurfacing of the churchyard at All Saints in Wellingborough, a (possibly Saxon) female skeleton was uncovered with several feet of plaited straw-coloured hair. The latter was subsequently taken to the vestry for safekeeping, but such an unusual find soon became a local talking point, so much so that inquisitive individuals, not without an element of superstition, began to help themselves to a few strands, reducing it over a period of time until nothing was left.

When houses were being demolished in 1960 along Church Street in the village of Corby, six inscribed stone slabs of masonry were retained, put in storage and, five years later, put on display on a wall behind the reception desk at the newly built town civic centre in 1965, together with datestones from other demolished buildings, all of them historic symbols of a fast-disappearing village at the mercy of the growing new town on its doorstep. After the civic centre was also pulled down in 1999, the slabs were given a temporary home at East Carlton Park and earmarked for display in the new heritage centre, which opened in 2011.

What was so special about the six slabs? There was an air of mystery about their provenance and why they had been used in such a manner. They were inscribed in Latin as follows: 'NATA 1619, SEPULTA 1638, RESURGENDA' ('born 1619, buried 1638, she must rise again'); 'NEMO SCIT, NE ANGELI, NE FILIUS' ('no one knows, neither the angels, nor the son'); 'MEA FILIA' ('my daughter'); 'USQUE QUO DIVE?' ('how long, oh Lord?'); 'HIC OPERIS FINIS, NON DOLORES' ('here was the end of my work, but not my sorrow'); 'AUDIO VIATOR, SI HABES LIBEROS, HABES LINDE, SAEPE MORI POSSIS' ('listen traveller, if you have children you have whereof, you can often die'). What would have been a seventh piece recording the girl's name has never been traced.

Part of the ledger of Bridget Twickten, later broken up for house construction in Corby village.

Who was she? Later investigations and research uncovered her identity and more. She was Bridget Twickten, who had died tragically young before her nineteenth birthday, possibly from one of the many epidemics so commonplace in that age. She was the daughter of John Twickten, the rector of the parish church of Corby from 1614 to 1657, who had been a great benefactor to the village, leaving many gifts to the poor, including the provision of a Bible bound with the inscription 'The gift of Dr Twickten [to] every household that can read or hath a child that can read'.

So attached had he been to the village during his lengthy incumbency that in his will (1657) John Twickten stated, 'I desire to be buried either in the grave of my deare daughter, or close to the grave of my sonne.' His son, also John, had died in 1655, and his wife had followed in 1661. There are presently four ledgers in the floor of the chancel of the church of St John the Baptist, two either side of the altar: those of John senior and his son on one side, his wife Ann and an unmarked stone on the other. This may well be where Bridget is buried, but why it is unmarked is a mystery, as is why her original stone had been removed and broken up.

Sometimes a headstone can be found with the inscription side facing a boundary wall, often placed so close that the wording (if any) is impossible to read, as is the case at Newton, where the headstone is sited west of the porch, by the churchyard entrance. A similarly placed headstone can be found at Blatherwycke, although in this case there is a small gap that enables the inscription to be read, albeit with great difficulty. In this instance, however, the name of the deceased can be seen, together with lengthy funerary verse. It refers to a black servant, Anthony Williams, who in 1836 jumped into a lake to save the life of his master, who had fallen off a boat while fishing. He succeeded, but was not so lucky himself, drowning during the rescue. Another black servant who performed a similar heroic act was James Chapple, who had saved his master, Christopher Hatton IV, while staying at a castle in Guernsey during a storm. In gratitude, Hatton retired his servant with a generous pension to his manor at Gretton, where he resided at one of the village hostelries. He is said to have been buried in the churchyard, yet there is no grave marker. Perhaps, like so many other people, he was unable to afford such a 'luxury'. In both cases, however, these anomalies may be a form of racial prejudice.

The twelfth-century tomb lid now seen in the church of St Peter in Northampton disappeared for several years before finally being returned to its original provenance in 1932 after going through a series of other uses, first resurfacing as a lintel for the door of a nearby cottage during the 1840s, then as a mantelpiece in the boardroom of a nearby brewery. At Rothwell, two thirteenth-century tomb lids were found during restoration of the church tower roof in 1981. They had lain there for nearly 500 years; each weighed about half a ton. They were consequently lowered down to the ground by special crane, and can now be seen in the south aisle. 'Recycling' items like this is not unusual; in at least one case, a tomb lid is known to have been used as means of crossing a stream.

One of the strangest monuments to appear in the county was the Volta Tower at Finedon, a tall, ornate, castellated folly that was built by the lord of the manor, William Mackworth Dolben, as a memorial to his son, who had died at sea off the coast of West Africa in April 1863. It became a dwelling until it spectacularly collapsed in 1951, killing one of the occupants.

The 100-foot-high Boughton Obelisk was another monumental 'folly' built in the previous century. Still standing today – some might say precariously close to neighbouring houses – it was erected with a 1764 memorial inscription by William Wentworth, in memory of his great friend the Duke of Devonshire.

Mention must also be made of the two ornate Eleanor crosses in the county, standing at Geddington and Hardingstone (near Delapré Abbey), both constructed in around 1294. They are two of only three surviving crosses; twelve were erected after the premature death of Queen Eleanor, who died in Harby, Nottinghamshire, in December 1290. They were set up at each of the overnight resting places of the funeral cortège making its way from Lincoln to London for her burial at Westminster Abbey. They are unique in being among the earliest examples of the new Decorated Period 'micro-architecture' in England, based on the commemorative monuments of Louis IX of France that had been constructed twenty years earlier.

In the north chapel of the church of St Mary Magdalene at Yarwell is an ornate limestone-panelled altar tomb with a black marble top, which has a deeply engraved carving of a wild man (a symbol of protection and strength). It is the tomb of Humphrey Bellamy, a prosperous merchant and former alderman of London who died in 1715. There is a village tradition that he came there as a sick and destitute boy, whereupon he was clothed, fed and nursed back to health by the community and made his way to London to seek his fortune, which he duly did (in some ways, his is similar to the story of Dick Whittington). In his old age, Bellamy returned to the village to spend his last days and endowed a charity to support the poor in gratitude for the care he had once been given.

Two unique headstones along a riding in a secluded spinney at Deene mark the place where a local man proposed to his sweetheart, and where they were later buried side by side after years of happy marriage.

In the south aisle of the church of St Margaret at Crick, there is a late-eighteenth-century 'parson's hutch', the purpose of which was to shelter the parson from the elements while he conducted funeral services.

An unusual burial took place in the churchyard at Oundle in 1909, when a nine-year-old boy, Frank Burnham Wood, was buried in a coffin covered in white velvet.

Something of a mystery occurred at Kingscliffe in November 1799, when Hannah Faulkner, a village widow and travelling pedlar, was interred in a barn without a service or even the tolling of a bell. The circumstances are unknown, and certainly unusual, provoking a comment in *The Gentleman's Magazine* in February 1800.

A former farmer's wife at Cogenhoe is said to have had frugal habits, despite not wanting for anything. She was known for searching the dustbins of her neighbours for scraps of food for her husband's meals. She was also the 'layer out' of corpses in the village, and it was said that her mouth could not close properly due to her oversized false teeth, which were supposedly sourced from the corpses in her care.

'GIANTS'

Daniel Lambert, 52 st 11 lbs at the time of his death, was, in his lifetime, the heaviest man ever recorded. Born in March 1770, he became keeper of Leicester Prison for four years before he began travelling around the country, charging a shilling a head to those who sought an audience with him. He subsequently came to the Wagon and Horses at Stamford St Martin, on the Northamptonshire side of the River Welland. Unable to gain access to the upper floor due to his immense girth, he took apartments on the ground floor. This is where he died, which subsequently led to logistical problems: in attempting to remove him from the hostelry, the wall and window of his room had to be dismantled. The *Stamford Mercury* reported the difficulties of placing him in his coffin, which had to be rectangular in order to accommodate the body, the legs alone 'being of immense substance'. The newspaper mentioned the coffin as measuring 6 feet 4 inches in length, 4 feet 4 inches in width, and 2 feet 4 inches in depth. It was constructed using '112 superficial feet of elm, built on two axle trees and four cog wheels'. It added, 'Upon these the poor man will be rolled into his grave at the new burial ground at the back of St Martin's church. A regular descent will be made by cutting away the earth for some distance.'

When an altar tomb was being removed during rebuilding of the church of St Margaret at Alderton, a giant figure in a stone coffin dating from the reign of Henry III (1216–72) was discovered underneath. Subsequent investigations led to the belief that it was a local knight who had been on the losing side (that of the rebel Simon de Montfort) at the Battle of Evesham in 1265 – the decisive engagement of the Second Barons' War, during which Henry III was taken prisoner. The knight is said to have been one of the survivors who had begged for mercy from the victor, the future King Edward I.

In many cases, however, we will never know the names of the occupants of more ancient tombs. Two stone coffins were discovered on church land at Blatherwycke in the late eighteenth century and now reside in the garden of the former rectory. When opened, they were found to contain the remains of a very tall female skeleton, the upper half (from the knees upwards) in one, the lower portion together with a pottery vessel in the other. The remains possibly dated from the Romano-British era, and theories began to circulate as to the identity of the occupant, the wildest one being that it was Boudicca, Queen of the Iceni, who had been defeated by Roman forces near Mancetter in around AD 60. (Perhaps being tall was among the criteria for acquiring regal status.) Females of great stature, however, are not that uncommon – several have been found in Anglo-Saxon graves in the county. In the porch of the now-derelict church of St Mary in Arden, just inside the county boundary of Leicestershire, there is the mutilated stone effigy of an unknown 1.8-metre (6 feet 6 inches) female.

CREMATION

Cremation was practised intermittently in England until the end of the pagan Saxon era. Thereafter it was rejected for centuries by the Christian Church, which saw the body as a sacred entity and a necessary prerequisite for resurrection on the Day of Judgment. (In medieval superstition, the image of a skull and crossbones, like the body itself, was a prerequisite for resurrection.) Only those people whose souls were deemed to be damned – heretics and traitors – had their bodies cremated, albeit as the death penalty for their crimes. It was not until the later years of the nineteenth century that a new philosophy and attitude led to its use as an alternative to inhumation. It became the dominant form of burial in the second half of the twentieth century and beyond.

This change of attitude was partly one of necessity. As the population grew through the years, multiple burials, lack of space for interments, overcrowding and poor sanitation led to contamination of the earth and water supply, which led to a host of infections and epidemics, such as cholera, dysentery, and typhoid, all of which came to a head in the nineteenth century. Opening up cemeteries or extending churchyards where possible was one answer, but a more simple and economical (even eco-friendly) method of solving the problem was cremation. It is human nature to dislike and resist change – witness today's protests against public spending cuts, proposed housing or industrial development, and wind farms – but it eventually became an attractive alternative.

The first crematorium in England was built in 1879 at Woking in Surrey, with the first *legal* cremation taking place there six years later. Northamptonshire was somewhat slower in adopting the idea, but 'the Counties Crematorium' for the Northampton district was opened by the Bishop of Peterborough at Milton Malsor in July 1939, followed by the Kettering Crematorium in April the following year.

4

THE ART OF DYING

This ae night, this ae night,
Every night and alle,
Fire and fleet and candle light,
And Christ receive thy saule.

If hosen and shoon thou ne'er gav'st nane,
Every night and alle,
The whinnies shall prick thee to the bane,
And Christ receive thy saule.

If ever thou gavest meat and drink,
Every night and alle,
The fire shall never make thee shrinke,
And Christ receive thy saule.

(From the medieval *Lyke-Wake Dirge*)

Before the Reformation, the biggest fear about dying was the thought of a long spell in Purgatory, that place/state of spiritual cleansing that preceded Heaven. Books such as *Ars Moriendi*, or 'The Art of Dying' (*c.* 1416), and *The Arte and Crafte to Lyve Well and to Dye Well* by Wynkyn de Worde (1505) were highly influential illustrated works, chastising and admonishing the masses and showing them what to expect in Purgatory, but also acting as guides on how to ease their passage and shorten the length of time they spent in misery and despair. However, repentance and prayers made on the deathbed were not enough – more preferable were charitable actions carried out during the lifetime while in good health and with a genuine sense of care and concern. Whether they had done works of goodwill during their lives or not, those with sufficient means usually made some form of provision *after* their death, as any gift was seen as the most powerful and selfless form of charity. The most common entries in such bequests were for the repair, maintenance or beautification of the church, such as:

- 'To the churche of Okley Parva, a bord clothe of dyaper worke to make ij awter clothes, oon to the hie aulter and a nother to our Lady's aulter.' (J. Decons, 1530)
- 'To bye a banner clothe, iiij*s*. iiij*d*.' (Thomas Stobley, Stanion, 1531)
- 'To the sepulchre light, xij*d*.' (Richard Alambe, Corby, 1522)
- 'To the byldyng of the stepull, xxi*s*. viii*d*.' (Robert Parker, Rothwell, 1528)
- 'To the Reparacon of St Edmonds Altar and Chapell, xx*d*.' (Philip Powel, Oundle, 1531)
- 'Towards the paynting of Saynt Margaret.' (Edward Sanderson, Wadenhoe, 1519)

'LIGHTS' AND 'TORCHES'

In bequests, there are frequent references to 'lyghtes'. These were candles and tapers provided to accompany images of saints in their respective altars or chapels, and for the top of the rood screen that separated the chancel from the nave. Here they would continually illuminate the images of the cross with the Virgin Mary and St John on either side.

However, 'torches', also known as 'serges', were different from wax lights both in fabric and use. They were larger, thicker and, not being of pure wax, brown in colour, due to the resin added during their manufacture. They were placed by the side of a body during funeral rites and the requiem mass. The wealthy stipulated they be provided primarily for their own funeral, but also to the church for the benefit of the community. Many churches had their own supply for burying the poor, and for use during special occasions. Apart from being symbols of light, life and renewal, blessed candles were seen as yet another powerful evil-averting tool.

The average cost was half a noble or 3*s* 4*d*, which would be left in the form of money or grain. Pre-Reformation bequests reflected this provision, and usually in English, which was beginning to replace Latin in many official documents. With no formalised spelling at the time, this was written according to dialect or guesswork, so that some quaint words appear, such as 'cowpull' (couple), 'pisshen' (parish), 'bye' (buy) and 'oone' (one). Note that the word 'herse' did not have the same meaning as the modern word 'hearse'; it was a general word applied to a temporary monument/framework for housing the body or effigy of a wealthy individual, and was placed above the burial plot for the duration of the funeral service (the origin of the word being from an old French word for 'rake' or 'harrow'). It was a tent or gable-like structure with a pall cover and was surrounded by 'torches'. Sometimes, however, after being given a covering of lead or other metal, it could be permanent, with one known example in the county being recorded at Spratton (1371).

There was a standard accounting system at the time, with money being reckoned in shillings and pence, using Latin numerals with a final 'i' written as a 'j' (for example, 4*d* was written as iiij*d*). Measures and quantities were given (using now-antiquated names), the most common being a 'strike' (or half a bushel), which was equivalent to four gallons. The following list gives a flavour of this type of bequest from around the county:

- 'To every torche that shall be at my herse, ij*d*.' (J. Andrew, West Haddon, 1531).
- 'I bequeath to by iiij torches with, and to lyghte one at my burying, iijs, iiij*d*.' (Thomas Berde, Cransley, 1521)
- 'I beqeth ij pounds of waxe to be made in serges and to be set about my herse on the day of my burying.' (J. Adcocke, Glapthorne, 1512).
- 'I bequeath to the maintenance of the torchis, a stryke of barley.' (Thomas Kenersley, Syresham 1528)
- 'So miche money as will by oone torche, the wiche I will be used yn the administracon of the blessed sacrament and at pore mens buryalls.' (J. Pye, Walgrave, 1530)
- 'To the torchys, a quarter of malt.' (Thomas Bosynghoo, Stoke Bruerne, 1514)
- 'Item, to bye a torch into ye chyrch, iijs.' (Richard Court, Pattishall, 1513).
- 'To the churche ij torchis of waxe, in wayght xiij powndes.' (Richard Cross, Church Brampton, 1528)

Another bequest, at Helmdon in 1523, left a 'stryke of barley to the torche ale'.

Sometimes, instead of money left for the provision of candles, the wax for making the candles was itself donated, as shown in the following examples. Richard Wolaston of Aldwincle St Peter (*d.* 1527) left 'Joane Dravuter' his bee hives, with the following proviso: 'I will that halfe the wax of these bee hyves shalbe brent in the churche for me and all Christen soules aslonge as they will endure.' Robert Malarye of Geddington (*d.* 1529) left 'to the hye aulter, a hyve full of beys an waxe'.

THE POOR AND THE COMMUNITY

Also of crucial importance was some form of donation to the less fortunate members of the community, usually in the form of money – a penny or twopence 'per poor person' being the norm – or fuel for heating. One particular villager living at Old stipulated that a load of wood was to be distributed among the villagers on his decease, while Myles Ros of Naseby requested: 'every house in the parish to have a cheese, and the poorest house, the best cheese'. John Cranfield of Harlestone said, in 1558, 'Every Crosse Monday yearly 8*d* to be drunken amonge the poore.'

The prayers of the poor were considered to be particularly effective in strengthening the cause of the deceased in his mission, and if a large number of such people could be enlisted to attend the funeral as 'weepers', so much the better. This would be encouraged with the promise of alms for all of those who came along to stand around the grave, hold candles and join in the prayers:

John Naylor, Rothwell stipulated in 1522: 'my wife to bring me honestlye to the church with xij pore folks barying in thyr hands one taper of waxe being of half a li [half a pound] apece'.

In 1487, Margaret Brafeld, a wealthy Northampton widow, gave detailed instructions for her burial in the chapel of Corpus Christi at the church of All Saints, including: 'I will that the said executors order at my own expense, 13 wax torches, each containing 13 lbs wax in weight, to be burnt around my body on the day of my burial, during my exequies, and sung or spoken requiem mass as bequested ... 13 poor people to hold the said torches, both at my exequies and also at my Mass and burial ... 13 gowns to be had and applied to the use of the poor for ever.'

Sometimes there was a desire to have as many members of the community present as possible, regardless of status, for the greater number of voices heard at prayer would also help the cause of the deceased. To ensure this, a certain amount of generosity was once again involved.

Edward Martin of Old in 1544: 'to be brewed (for) a burial. 4 quarters of malt, 3 bullocks, 6 sheep, 3 calves, 6 pigs, hens and capons, as need shalbe and were to be prepared for the same together with 3 quarters of "bred corne" that all comers might be relyvyd.'

Agnes Basilye of Hellidon (*d.* 1546): 'iij dosen of brede and chese and ale convenient to be eten and drunken after masse of the people being present in giving God thanks and praying for my soule.'

Miles Ros of Naseby (*d.* 1529) was particularly generous, with two other bequests, both aimed at tempting members of the community to attend his funeral. Firstly: 'every person that shall be at my beryall shall have ij*d*'. Secondly: 'I wyll that ther be ij blake clothes with white crosses on my grave, and on my wyvis [wife's] and ther on to be sett ij sergis to bren [torches to burn] att all masses that shall be sayd for me and my wyve and all massis at the hy auter during one yere ... iij dosen of brede and chese and ale convenient to be eten and drunken after masse, of the people being present in giving God thanks and praying for my soule.'

Sometimes bequests might include something charitable for the good of the community in general – something that would contribute to its overall well-being and comfort. This was usually money given for the repair and/or maintenance of a bridge or highway, a typical example being that of Thomas Angiers of Paulerspury, who bequested in 1532, 'one half of my goodes to be spente in works of mercye as in mendyng of the hiewayes'.

At Cottesbrooke, John Handros, a 'weyfayryngman' who had repaired the rood loft and ordered decorative material for it, left a bequest, but with a proviso in 1533: 'I gyff the townshippe of Cottesbroke the seide golde sylver byse oyle [with] all other thing thereto belong, so that thei paye me iiij nobles more for to pay me ber[ying] and to reward them that take peyne with me in my syknes.'

However, perhaps the most generous of all benefactors in the county was a very wealthy townsman, Thomas Bukke of Northampton, who was buried at the church of St Giles in 1479, and left vast sums of money to twenty-four other churches, all in the north of the county where he had been born. Sums varied between 3*s* 4*d* and 10*s*, with Wilbarston receiving a generous £1 6*s* 8*d* for the 'hygh awter' and 'reparacon' of the church. Sums were left for the poor of each of the villages, varying from a standard 3*s* 4*d* to the 6*s* 8*d* (half a mark) given to Wilbarston (again) and Rothwell. Money was also left to repair the bridges of Cottingham, Rockingham, Harringworth, Rothwell, Desborough, Weston by Welland, Ashley and others in the vicinity. In addition, large sums were left for the nuns of Rothwell, all orders of friars in Stamford and Northampton, the nuns of Stamford and Northampton, the poor men of St Thomas and St John in Northampton, and 12*d* for each 'pore person in the towne of Northampton'.

ALES

Another way of giving something to the community was leaving something towards the brewing of ale and the provision of food for special occasions such as the annual beating the bounds of the parish during Rogation Week, or for the upkeep of the church. The following bequests give some idea of the deceased's generosity:

- 'To the church ayll, j stryke of whete.' (T. Browks, Helmdon, 1528)
- 'To the church ale at Whitsontyde, haullf a quarter of mallt.' (W. Synkyn, Towcester, 1523)
- 'To the Young Men's Ale at Myddelton, ij busshell of malt.' (W. Stanley, Warkworth, 1560)
- 'One cow left to the churchwardens to make a drynkynge wt in the procession weeke.' (John Heycock, Long Buckby)
- 'Bred and beere in Crosse Month at the discretion of the churchwardens so long as the world endureth.' (Thomas Rowell, Cottingham, 1559, funded by income from his house)
- 'I guyff a red heckfor to the procession ale on Weymsdaye in the Rogation weeke.' (James Wyatt, Deene, 1532)
- 'I will ther shall be prepared agaynst my buriall in the churche of Lilford for my moulde ale in bred and drink 3 shillinges and fouer pence.' (Robert Mell, Lilford, 1557)

THE CUSTOM OF 'MORTUARY'

Whenever anyone of a certain means died, an early form of 'death duty' was imposed. It was customary for the deceased to give his 'best beast' (usually an ox) as a gift to the lord of the manor, and his 'second best beast' to the priest (although it was forbidden under canon law for him to receive such a 'gift' unless the deceased owned at least three beasts). The 'gift' was also known as a 'corse-present' or 'fore-drove', the latter name deriving from the original practice of the beast being led at the head of the funeral procession. There were later variations, especially after the Black Death, when only the priest or another religious authority was the recipient. Sometimes other gifts were donated in lieu, such as an item of jewellery, a gown, a cloak or a hood. Bequests often referred to the gift as being given 'according to the custome of the towne'. Examples from around the county include:

- 'I bequeath to the curate my best beste, to pray for me and to recyve non other thynge for my mortuarye.' (John Mason, husbandman of Irchester, 1532)

- '... for my mortuary, my best good wych in a black awmlyng horse, after the manner of the towne'. (William Drage of Higham Ferrers, 1512)
- 'To the vicar of Seynt Gyles, Northampton, where I am dwelling, for my mortuary, my best jewell, after the custom of the towne.' (Margaret Harrowden, 1485)
- '... my sinfull body to be buryed in the chauncell of Blakesley ... I bequest to Master Nicholas Clarke the best cowe that I have yf the Bishop doe not chose hur.' (Alex Hyde, priest at Blakesley, 1529)

There was also another form of payment, supposedly voluntary but expected, known as an 'oblation', which was a small fee given to the priest for a burial. This and the mortuary disappeared during the Reformation, with only a slight relapse during the reign of Mary I, but in a weakened form, before it permanently disappeared in around 1559. Such a practice was anathema to Protestant reformers and the public in general.

SPECIAL REQUESTS AND MASSES

Occasionally there were deviations from the standard contents of a bequest, with special instructions to be carried out either at the time of burial, or for a period thereafter. One of the most interesting is that of Henry Godwin of Irchester (*d.* 1526), who showed great humility in the way he wished to be buried:

> To be buryed next unto holy water stoke [stoup] as may be so the people may tredde and come over my grave and sepulture.

Others might be more elaborate:

- 'I will that a waxe taper shall stande upon my grave & shall burne at hie masse tyme every daye that masse shalbe saide or songe thoroghe & for a hole yere after my decesse.' (John Heydon, Edgcote, 1545)
- 'Unto a Clarke peyng a graduatt to saye a sarmen in the sayd churche of Flowre at the day of my burial, vjs. iiijd.' (Philippa Mechyll, Flore, 1527)

In 1379, John Pyel of Irthlingborough willed that his body 'be covered de blanket et de russet [white and red], one taper at his head, another at his feet ... thirteen poor folk clothed in blanket and russet to hold 13 torches during the mass when his body shal be buried ...'

 A number of special masses had their origins in various visions and revelations to holy men by heavenly figures. Among these was that of the 'Five Wounds', commemorating the five wounds Christ suffered while he was hanging on the cross (the fifth being the lance piercing the body to ensure that no life remained). While an unspecified Pope Benedict lay dying, the Archangel Raphael is said to have appeared and ordered him to write down the words of a mass and to say the text five times, one for each wound, whereupon he made a full recovery. It became a mass for assisting the soul's passage into heaven, and was considered one of the most solemn ceremonies of all. Four county examples here show its relative popularity in the pre-Reformation period:

- 'I will that Sir Robert, curat of Paykyrke sey for me v messys of the feyve wondys.' (Margaret Herbe, Glinton, 1511)
- 'A priest to say v massys of the v wounds, xx*d*.' (W. Phylip, Lutton, *c*. 1515)
- 'For v massys of ye v wounds of our Lord Jhs Christe ... at ye disposition of my gostly father for ye helth of my soule, xx*d*.' (Thomas Stanton, Harlestone, 1521)
- 'I bequeth to say v masses to the v pryncypall wondes of our Lord, xx*d*.' (Sir Thomas Cheney, Bulwick, *c*. 1520)

Another mass, the *Scala Coeli* ('Ladder of Heaven'), has its origins in around 1138. While St Bernard of Clairvaux was celebrating mass, he had a vision of angels leading the souls of the dead out of Purgatory into Heaven along a ladder. The miraculous event caused widespread excitement and led to an oratory in Rome taking on the name of Santa Maria Scale Coeli and becoming a centre for celebration of the story. With the concept of Purgatory – and the need to shorten the time spent there – in the minds of the wealthier element of society, the mass would have struck a chord, and was not forgotten in bequests such as that of Margaret Phyllypes of Brigstock (*d*. 1521), who stipulated, 'v masses to be caused to be sayd at the *scala coeli*'. Sir Thomas Cheney of Bulwick asked for five masses 'of *Scala Celi*'.

However, since a journey to Rome for this purpose was impractical, a major religious centre in the homeland such as Westminster or Oxford was often chosen. J. Benett (*d*. 1522): 'a Trentall of masses done for my soul at Scala Celi in Oxford'. Trental masses, a series of thirty set requiems celebrated over a thirty-day period or a year, were believed to be of additional benefit to souls during their stay or 'captivity' in Purgatory. As part of the process, the priest carrying out the ceremony had to fast or wear a coarse shirt every Friday during the period. The origin of the masses is said to have been established in 1410 by Pope Gregory, after his dead mother appeared to him in a terrifying form and confessed a great sin she had secretly committed in the early years of her life: the infanticide of her illegitimate child. After urging him to say thirty masses, she miraculously took on a holy form resembling that of the Virgin Mary. The masses subsequently became known as the Trental of St Gregory.

Another popular medieval requiem mass was that of the Month Minde, celebrated a month after the burial of the deceased in his or her memory. It was usually accompanied by some form of feasting, and was an English Christian adaptation of an ancient Saxon and Viking custom of a drinking ceremony in memory of the dead. The requiem mass took place throughout the medieval period and into the Tudor era. The word still exists in Scandinavia – and Lancashire – as 'minde' or 'minna', meaning 'memory'. One such example in Northamptonshire is that of Stephen Euxton of Lois Weedon (*d*. 1524): 'Also yf God of hys grett gudnes do hys wyll by me at this tyme, I wyll to have a drynkyng for my soll health all my moneth myned yn my parysh of Lewys Wedon.'

'*De Profundis*' also featured in bequests. This was a set of penitentials, with an emphasis on the Psalms and the Litany of the Saints, that was seen as crucial during intercession for the dead, giving them extra fortitude to bear the burden of Purgatory. Its origin lay in the opening words of the Latin Psalm 130 (it translates as 'out of the depths'). An example from the county, with particular generosity – and persuasion – was the bequest of William Vyend of Harrington (*d.* 1542):

> A cowe to the maintenance of a drynkyng at Axys crosse, or at the Frythe lane, one the Monday in the Rogacion processyon week, under the condycon that Mr Vicar shall say De Profundis for the sowls of his father and mother and for all Christen sowls, the vicar to have for hys labor a cake and a pott with ale ...

BEDE ROLLS

Parish bede rolls came into being *c.* 1500, and were lists of persons who had given gifts to the church and/or the poor. Being on the list enabled them to be prayed for over a set period of years, 'perpetually by name so as not to be forgotten', but it still needed some form of 'insurance' for this to happen, requiring a large sum of money because of the timescale. For example, John Elmes of Lilford left £56 13s for the purpose 'vjli xiijs so that the inhabitants of Lylford put me in the bedroll [*sic*] by the space of 20 yeres and to cause me to be prayd for especyally'.

CHANTRY BEQUESTS

Chantries were small foundations set up to support a priest to say daily or regular mass for the soul of a benefactor and his family. They were either based in part of an existing church (e.g. at Rushton All Saints, the chantry of St Mary's, 1268), or were specially built chapels in or close to the churchyard, as was the case at Easton on the Hill (1293), Harringworth (as at All Saints', 1304), and Bulwick (as at St Mary and St Anne, *c.* 1390).

Collegiate churches were a larger type of establishment, usually attached to an existing church, and had a closed community 'living in'. As well as acting as a chantry, they performed additional duties like a monastery, catering for the sick and the poor. There were five in the county: at Cotterstock, Fotheringhay, Higham Ferrers, Irthlingborough and Towcester (with a sixth organised on a different basis by a group of town priests under a warden at All Saints', Northampton).

Cotterstock had been founded in 1340 by John Gifford, provost and lord of the manor, who had been in the service of Queen Isabella, wife of Edward III, and had held the important position of steward of her lands 'beyond the Trent'. It was attached to the church of St Andrew and consisted of Gifford in charge as provost, twelve priests and two clerks, and acted as a chantry for Gifford, his brother, Edward III and Isabella. At Fotheringhay, the college was originally founded in 1398 in the chapel of the castle by the first Duke of York, Edmund Langley, and his son, before moving to the church of St Mary the Virgin and All Saints in 1411, taking over the site of a nunnery that had relocated to Delapré in Northampton. It consisted of the provost, eight clerks and thirteen choristers, and as time went by masses were said for the souls of Richard II, Henry IV, Henry V, and their families.

At Irthlingborough, the lord of the manor (and Lord Mayor of London) John Pyel arranged for a chantry college to be set up, something which came to fruition after his death, thanks to his wife Joan. It was attached to the church of St Peter in 1388. Six secular chaplains (one of whom was the dean) and four clerks were employed in saying masses for the souls of the founders. At Higham Ferrers, Archbishop Henry Chichele set up his college in 1422 with eight secular canons or chaplains, eight clerks and six choristers, to pray for the souls of himself, Henry V, Henry's queen and parents, and 'all the faithful departed'. At Towcester, Archdeacon William Sponne, rector of the church of St Lawrence, set up a small chantry of two priests to sing for his soul.

RELIGIOUS GILDS

Fraternities and gilds (not to be confused with trade guilds) were a common feature of towns and certain villages, playing an important role in the social and religious life of the community. There were eight in the church of All Saints in Northampton alone. They were composed of groups of leading townspeople, male and female, who regularly came together for various purposes, and had their own special feast day, annual procession, and a dedicated priest, altar and chapel in a designated part of the church, or in close proximity. One particular gild at Oundle, that of St Mary, in the church of St Peter, was founded by Joan Wyatt in 1498–99, and was served by two chaplains, and there was also an associated gild house standing near the church. Its popularity can be seen in several bequests:

- '... to the wardens of the Gild of Our Lady at Owndell, a cow'. (John Rawlynse of Warmington, 1499)
- A sum of money left 'to the gild of Our blessyd lady for to make ii husbands and myself, bred'n, and systorn of the seid gild'. (Agnes Dobbs, 1514)
- '... to the gylde of Our laydie towdyd in Oundell my byggst brasse pot for my neweltie'. (Ellen Faulkner, 1531, annual payment)

BENEFACTORS' TABLETS

No pockets in shrouds.

(An old Northamptonshire saying)

Following the Reformation, provision for the poor was encouraged even more than it had been before. Annual doles of money or bread became commonplace in ensuing years, at a prescribed time and place, usually by the grave of the benefactor or in the church porch, as on May Day at Geddington (still continued in modified form today)

A wooden board in the church of St Mary at Wappenham with details of a local benefactor's bequest.

and at Great Oakley, where alms from the Andrew Pymill charity were distributed to the seven poorest persons on St Andrew's Day (in November).

Benefactors' tablets can be seen in many churches around the county, often in the south aisle above the doorway or on the walls of the tower. One of the most unusual was that of Thomas Coles of Blatherwycke (*d.* 1684), who willed that a piece of land be set aside, the rent from which would enable six of the poorest men in the village to receive a 'plum pudding' annually on Christmas Day. Income for the poor raised from the rental of a piece of land (or provision of land for use by the poor) was not uncommon in future years, as the following field names testify: Poor's Lot at Weston, Poor Close at Sibbertoft, Poor's Close at Greatworth, Poorman's Sale at Deene, Poor's Piece at Aynho, and Charity at Kislingbury. Such names also came into being during the eighteenth-century Enclosure Awards and the Select Vestry Acts of 1819 and 1831, the latter providing Brington with 'the Poor's Allotment'.

One of the most generous benefactors in the county was Jane Leeson, a spinster who lived in Abthorpe and died in 1648. Six years earlier, she had built the village school (now the village hall). A stone tablet can be seen on the wall facing the street, inscribed, 'Jane Leeson hath builded this house as a free school for ever. Fear God, honor ye king, 1642.' (Adding these latter words was perhaps a daring thing to do in the year the

English Civil War broke out.) In her will she gave sums of money to the poor of the area, ranging from £3 for Abthorpe, £1 10s for Paulerspury and Wappenham, and £1 each for neighbouring villages such as Syresham, Alderton, Silverstone and Whittlebury. A later benefactor's tablet that included her name (possibly a replacement) was set up in the village church in 1737. At neighbouring Wappenham, however, is an earlier tablet recording her generosity:

> Mrs Jane Leeson, spinster, late of Abthorp in the Parish of Towcester gave for ever the sum of one Pound ten Shillings to this Parish which said is to be received annually of the Trustees of this Charity by the Rector and churchwardens for the time being and distributed among ye Poor hereof, especially old Maids and Widows according to their Discretion upon St Thomas Day.

Benefactors' tablets continued to be placed in churches until the end of the nineteenth century and there are a great number of these to be found such as that of Anne Reeve at Yelvertoft. In August 1866, she left £200 to be invested in funds, the interest from which was to pay for coal to be distributed annually to those of the poor 'who were most in need'.

Perhaps the most magnanimous bequest of all was that of Jemima Creed, who in 1706 gave the village of Ashton (near Oundle) a chapel, school and meadow. The benefactor's tablet in the chapel also has her portrait set in a roundel.

5

WRITTEN IN STONE

I wandered mid the surrounding graves,
Where coarse rank weedy herbage waves,
Musing of those who slept below,
Their tales of joy, or hope, or woe.

(A. W. Brown, *Lyrical Poems*)

... we gaze around:
We read their monuments; we sigh; and while
We sigh, we sink; and are what we deplor'd;
Lamenting, or lamented, all our lot!

(Edward Young, *Night-Thoughts*, 1742–44)

Headstones and other monuments are a valuable resource for social and local historians – one that is often overlooked. For centuries, the majority of burials were made *en masse* outside the church in unmarked graves. Sometimes there was a marker made of wood, but because of the impermanence of the material, these have long since perished. From the seventeenth century, stone markers became popular. They were crude in design at first, with basic wording, a date, and perhaps a simple skull or similar motif. They were small and usually flat-topped or wave-headed, until the following century when they became more substantial in size, with new forms having a curved or humped top. Some were carved in the lancet style, which imitated the pointed-arch windows of the Early English period. These were followed by round-topped, sinuous and shouldered forms. Gradually, they became more ornate and symbolic, sometimes with the mason's name at the base, and often including some funerary verse or more detailed information. Those in ironstone eroded very quickly, and even limestone tended to suffer from the elements over the years. Those made of slate in the 1800s (possible due to better transportation facilities) have proved to be the most durable.

There are a great many headstones around the county dating from the nineteenth century, mainly from the second half of the period, especially at Maidwell, Dodford, Greatworth, Weedon Lois and Culworth. The earliest surviving *legible* headstones, however, are at Duddington (1616, 1619 and 1642), Bugbrooke (1615 and 1643), and Easton on the Hill (1642).

Chest tombs also became increasingly popular. A few had made an appearance in earlier times, and by the fifteenth century they had coped lids and were ornamented with quatrefoils and shields on the side panels (as at Corby and Thrapston). The earliest legible later examples can be found at Wadenhoe (1592, 1637), Sulgrave (1632), Farthinghoe (1642), Weldon (1653), Great Oakley (1659, 1660), and Cottingham (1672). Thereafter they became very popular, particularly in the following century.

At the same time, flat gravestones (ledgers) inside the church became more numerous. An unusually early example, with a floriated cross and Lombardic lettering, is at Oundle for John de Owndell (*d.* 1278). Two others appeared as early as 1415 at Lowick and 1480 at Geddington, while two more made their appearance much later, at East Carlton in 1583 and Weldon in 1586. The earliest legible survivors from the seventeenth century can be found at Blatherwycke (1606), Barnwell All Saints (1611), Bulwick (1613), Oundle (1615), Yarwell (1617), Weldon (1620, 1634), Benefield (1620), Wadenhoe (1625), East Carlton (1627, 1632), Collyweston (1635), Wakerley (1636, 1638), and Aldwincle All Saints (1642, 1643); after which there was a great increase in numbers elsewhere around the county.

LETTERING

Lombardic lettering first appeared in northern Italy in the eleventh century, in the form of decorative capitals from medieval manuscript alphabets and derived from ancient Roman cursive letters. It appears on some monuments in churches around the county. Formulaic medieval French using this form of lettering was often used for memorials before the Black Death, but after 1364 Latin or English was the norm. There is an excellent example in the county, at Easton on the Hill, in the form of an incised inscription in the sill of the window of the south aisle, to the lord of the manor, Sir Richard de Lindon (*d.* 1255) and his wife, Ivette, inscribed: 'LES: CORS: SIRE: RICHARD: DE: LINDONE: E DAME: IVETE: SA: FEME: GISENT: CI: PRIEZ: PVR LES: AMES: KE: DEVS: EN: EIT: MERCE.' In the same part of the church is a late thirteenth-century floor slab with part of an inscription in Lombardic lettering, again in medieval French: 'VOUS KE SUR MO REGARDEZ PAR CHARIT …' In the chancel at Oundle, another example of Lombardic lettering (in Latin) can be found, inscribed on the floor slab of John de Oundle, who died in 1278.

At Geddington, an inscription in Lombardic lettering and Latin skirts the bottom of the north wall of the chancel, then winds around the base of the altar, along the south wall of the chancel, and into the adjoining south chapel. The first inscription dates from 1369 and is in memory of William Glover, a former chaplain (*capellanis*) of the church. The second is that of Robert de Geytingtourne, who built the south chapel ('*fecit istum cancellum*') during the same century.

This style was superseded after 1350 by Gothic 'blackletter' lettering (*c.* 1150–1530), commonly used in books and manuscripts, and on brasses such as that of Elizabeth

A seventeenth-century ledger with jumbled wording at All Saints', Aldwincle.

Ffollett at Collyweston (1508), which, like so many inscriptions during the period, was now in English. This style gave way to so-called copperplate writing.

Many other church and churchyard inscriptions, however, were often crudely carved, the spacing misjudged, some of the longer words or names overlapping from one line onto the next. There was also the contraction or abbreviation of a word by omitting, shrinking or linking certain letters (ligature) to save space. Even the word order suffered on occasion. A good example can be found in the now-redundant church of All Saints at Aldwincle, where a small rectangular ledger is inscribed at one end: 'August 22, 1643, Fleetwood Ford Thomas Ford We Dy'd to Live.' At the other end: 'Buried Octo 1642 Thomas Ford ye sons of We Liv'd to Dye.' Spelling variations were not uncommon, there being no guide to standardised national spelling until Samuel Johnson produced the first definitive dictionary in 1755. Until then, spelling was often guesswork, written and carved as heard or pronounced, according to dialect. Yet mistakes still persisted, two notable cases being on headstones at Oundle, where the last three letters of the word 'months' have been misspelt, with a messy attempt made at correction. On a later headstone, of 1863, the word 'interred' has been misspelt.

There could also be some hesitancy or confusion on the part of the mason when carrying out his work. At Sudborough, such hesitancy is apparent on the headstone of seventeen-year-old John Tebbutt, who died in 1775, which has inscribed, 'A youth beneath this hollow'd earth is laid,/Who his last Debt to Nature paid,/Scarce had he seen the Eighteenth churching,/Ere he his fragil thread of Life had frayed.' On the border by the side of the wording, '18th' is engraved, as if in confusion – or error?

Example of swirling calligraphic ornamentation on an eighteenth-century slate headstone.

Practice marks may be found on headstones, such as that of Alice Clinkard (*d.* 1876) on the north side of the churchyard at Wadenhoe, where the mason has tried out his lettering and word formation at the base. Trial lettering and practice work can also be found on the back of headstones.

CALLIGRAPHY

It was in the eighteenth century, however, that the 'younger' art of calligraphy came into its own, in many cases highly artistic and ornamental in form, with scrolling, elaborate swirls, and curved and looped stokes, engraved not just by one or two specialist funerary masons, but also by people of other occupations such as parish clerks or schoolmasters who had writing skills. Robert Waddington of Clipston's fine handiwork was in great demand in many places and can be seen on headstones in the churchyard and in those of nearby villages such as Kelmarsh and Naseby, as well as in neighbouring Leicestershire.

The same century – and beyond – also saw the rising popularity of epitaph verse on many headstones and a number of chest tombs, usually inscribed for those who had died prematurely in some way. Some of these verses had their origins in the Renaissance period, whose emphasis on mortality continued into the seventeenth century via metaphysical poets such as Andrew Marvell, George Herbert and John Donne. Some of these verses would be selected and refashioned for contemporary tastes. Quotations from the Bible also began to appear during the latter part of the century. Contemporary literary works were also popular, especially those by Alexander Pope and the 'Graveyard Poets', whose number included William Cowper, Thomas Warton, James Thomson, Thomas Parnell,

Thomas Gray (renowned for his 'Elegy Written in a Country Churchyard', 1751) and Edward Young. The latter's *Night-Thoughts* (1742–45) was particularly influential; parts of it were used on the headstone of Anne Roe (née Coles) at Aldwincle All Saints:

> Be wise today; 'tis madness to defer;
> Procrastination is the thief of time;
> Beware what earth calles happiness; beware
> All joys, but joys that never can expire.
> Who builds on less than an immortal base,
> Fond as he seems, condemns his joys to death.

RHYMING EPITAPH VERSE

> Why do Marbles cover Dust
> And Monuments our Bodys keep?
> Because the things they have in Light
> Are not Dead, but laid to Sleep.
> (A floor brass inscription at Harrington)

Some epitaph verse during the eighteenth and nineteenth centuries was made up by local scholars and clerics familiar with and influenced by the work of poets past and present. Living within the community, they would often have first-hand knowledge of the families in the parish, and would be able to add a personalised touch to the epitaph of the individual concerned; or they could recommend a suitable epitaph from a range available for a particular circumstance (something like today's greeting cards), such as the premature death of a child or wife or someone with a long-tem affliction. Unlike the more formalised verse of the famous poets, these would be lighter in tone, but just as effective in putting a feeling or tribute across – and they would have a simple rhyme.

Some of these standardised epitaphs had their origins in earlier times, as in the sixteenth-century English ballad, 'Death and the Lady':

> The grave's the market place where all must meet,
> Both rich and poor as well as small and great.
> If life were merchandise that gold could buy,
> The rich would live, only the poor would die.

The first two lines subsequently appeared in seventeenth-century works like *Reliquae*, a book of twenty-five poems by Sir Henry Wotton (1568–1639), the second two lines in a comedy, *The Two Noble Kinsmen*, written jointly in 1613 by Shakespeare and his contemporary and rival John Fletcher (1579–1625), but published posthumously in 1634. It became more widely circulated in broadsheet form in the 1680s, and even featured in three operas between 1729 and 1737. The Kettering printer Thomas Dash (1777–1841) also circulated a version for the county (a copy of which is now in the British Library).

A modified form appeared on a number of headstones in, among other places, Brackley and Ecton between 1730 and 1770, Stanwick between 1730 and 1734, and Kettering in 1766:

> This world's a city, full of crooked streets,
> Death is the market place where all men meet.
> If life was merchandise and men could buy,
> The rich would always live, the poor would die.

A similar type of verse was also found (again) at Brackley, during the same period, to members of the Tooley family:

> Our life is nothing but a winter's day,
> Some only break their fast and so away,
> Others stay to dinner and depart full fed,
> The longest guest but sups and goes to bed,
> He's most in debt that lingers out the day,
> Who dies betimes, has less and less to pay.

Another popular epitaph, one in which the virtues and attributes of a newly deceased young wife were compared with those of certain women in the Bible, appeared inside the church of All Saints at Wilbarston in 1738, and at St Giles at Desborough in 1762. There is only a slight variation between them in the wording of the first line. Desborough's version is bracketed:

> Behind a silent Grave death now embrace,
> [Behold this silent grave which doth embrace]
> A virtuous wife with Rachel's comely face,
> Sarah's obedience, Lydia's open heart,
> Martha's care and Mary's better part.

During the same period a similar type of composition appeared at Hannington, with some names changed or added:

> Wouldst thou reader draw to life,
> The perfect copy of a wife,
> Read on then from shame redeem,
> That lost but honourable name,
> This was once in spirit a Jael,
> Rebecca in grace, in heart an Abigail,
> In works a Dorcas, to the Church a Hannah,
> And to her spouse, Susanah,
> Prudently simple, providently wary,
> To the world a Martha, and to heav'n a Mary.

CAUSES OF DEATH

> You say the fever's burning round and taking old and young
> Then Sister, learn to love the Lord, while you are young and strong
> Death has been here at Belton and taken three away
> He went to Tailor Turner's upon the Sabbath day.
>
> (From a rhyming letter written by farm labourer
> Henry Branston to his sister in 1862)

Death can occur in a variety of forms: natural causes, illness, epidemic, suicide, accident, execution, murder or combat. Memorial inscriptions give some idea of premature death via the age of the deceased. Sometimes they also give the cause of what was often a tragic death. The majority, however, give no indication of what caused a particular life – or group of lives – to be taken away so early.

The most common form of death, apart from natural causes, was epidemics, among which were smallpox, typhoid, cholera, and, in the winter, typhus and influenza. Continuous outbreaks of plague occurred throughout the centuries, with one particularly virulent epidemic affecting Northampton in the summer of 1605. One notable entry in the parish registers for the church of All Saints recorded members of one family seemingly wiped out within a few days of each other in August and September:

> Joane, daughter of John Haskott buryed xixth daye, Mattie another daughter was buryed xixth daye, both of infection. Sicelye the daughter of John Haskott, was buryed the 27th daye. John Haskott was buryed the 28th daye. Widow Haskott was buryed the xvjth daye.

The next really devastating pestilence which hit the country was the plague of 1637–38. In Northampton, travellers, pedlars, fairs, markets, courts and church attendance helped to swell the numbers of those contracting the disease, the worst period being between July and September, with a peak of forty-two deaths occurring in August. The situation had not been helped by a smallpox epidemic spreading from the north. London in particular had been badly hit and the more affluent of Northamptonshire, who had gone there to seek refuge from the plague, found that they had leapt from the frying pan into the fire. Examining those parish registers existing at the time can give us some idea of the number of deaths from a pestilence, although it is likely in some cases that the sheer volume of victims led to names being unrecorded. There are some records, however, that do mention events, such as the parish register of Old (Wold) for 1638:

> At this time the plague was in the towne of which these dyed, but it pleased Almightie God to turn from wrath to mercie, so yt there did not dye a long tyme after, blessed be His name.

But there was a sting in the tail when one of those who had looked after the sick succumbed shortly afterwards, as the entry for 24 September 1638 records: 'Ann Randall, a poor woman who did attend on ye infested, was buried.'

Worse followed nationally twenty-five years later with the outbreak of the so-called Great Plague of 1665. Figures for Northamptonshire show variations in the number of victims, Kettering for example, sustaining eighty deaths during the period. In Northampton, several plague victims were buried in the churchyard of St Katherine's (one of the town's 'lost' chapels and churches). Everywhere, churches were being fumigated in various ways to 'prevent infection', the most popular being the strewing of sweet 'erbes in ye pews', plus holly, juniper, salts and balsams. A tarred barrel lit inside the church was also considered effective, as were portable pans containing fire. The introduction of tobacco during the late sixteenth century provided an additional 'weapon' against the plague, for it was widely thought that the disease did not like the smoke and would keep away from wherever it was used.

CONSUMPTION

Until the twentieth century, the most consistently deadly disease was consumption, the pulmonary form of tuberculosis, which affected the lungs, and which hit both the poor and the prosperous, males and females, especially from the age of fourteen upwards, and was easily spread among those in close proximity with one another, primarily by coughing and sneezing. It accounted for a large number of deaths and reached a peak during the nineteenth century. Anything that could undermine the health – such as influenza, malnutrition, overwork, overcrowding and poor hygiene – could encourage the bacteria to attack and gradually wear the body down, causing it to 'waste away' with tiredness, loss of appetite, fever and loss of blood.

A look around any churchyard will show a substantial number of premature deaths from consumption, although it is not always stated in the inscriptions. Variations of a particular verse can be found all over the place, three examples being:

- 'A pale consumption gave the fatal blow,/The disease was sure, but the effect was slow.' (Kettering)
- 'Consumption deep,/Laid us asleep,/My dear brother and I,/Weep not dear friends in vain,/But hope its for our gain,/That we so young should die' (Pywell children, Weldon)
- 'Consumption sore/Long time I bore,/Physicians they were in vain,/Til God did please/To give me ease,/And cured me of my pain.' (Mary Ann Steanes, Sibbertoft, aged 20, 1835).

A headstone by the entrance to the churchyard at Easton on the Hill records the death, possibly from consumption, of two sisters, both barely in their twenties, who died within a year of each other: 'Ann Taylor, aged 21 years and 3 months, died 4 November 1859. Her sister, Elizabeth, aged 20 years and 9 months, died 21 October 1860.'

The disease decimated families, the young being particularly vulnerable, as was the case again at Sibbertoft, where the four daughters of John and Susanna Ore passed away in the same year. The first two died within a short time of each other in 1827: Susannah (eighteen) on 12 February, followed by Jane (fourteen) on 16 March. The eldest, Anne (twenty), followed on the same day as Jane, and within a week she was joined by the youngest, Sarah (thirteen) on 22 March 1827. The inscription on Susannah and Jane's headstone reads:

> Gay youths observe this scene where many weep,
> Four sisters soon in death together sleep,
> Religion mind while yet 'tis called today,
> Ere in the bud of life you're snatched away.
> How short the time in which you may repent,
> Then now improve the hours in mercy lent.

The inscription on Anne and Sarah's headstone reads:

> Farewell dear friends, we bid to each adieu,
> No longer time is giv'n to dwell with you,
> Thro' Christ our Lord with God we make our peace,
> Who call'd us hence and gave us sweet release.
> May he who bore our sins upon the cross,
> Your hearts sustain in every loss.

A similar tragedy occurred over at Great Easton. Of the four daughters of Daniel and Catherine Holland, Hannah (twenty) died first, on 22 April 1800. Her headstone is inscribed:

> As buds and leaves when dropt do fade away,
> So this young blooming Virgin did decay,
> A deep Consumption o'er her so prevail'd
> That Youth and Beauty, Health and Strength hath fail'd,
> But yet we hope though stript of earthly charm,
> Her soul's embraced in her Saviour's arms.

Next were Sarah (twenty-four) and Mary (twenty) who died on 6 and 7 April 1802 respectively:

> Let us wipe our eyes with the comfort and hope and change our grief into a charitable joy, the friends we mourn for are delivered from this world and all miseries, we so justly deplore, their bodies tremble no more, with the palsey, nor burn with the flame of a scorching fever, they are … for want of sleep, nor roll up and down in their uneasy beds, but quietly rest in their silent grave, till they rise again in glory.

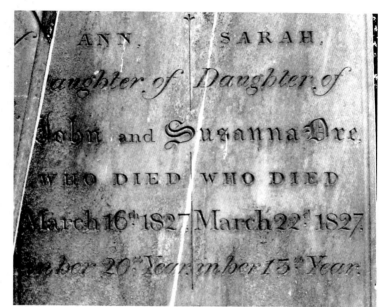

Inscriptions on one of two adjacent headstones at Sibbertoft, which record the premature deaths of the four Ore sisters.

The last to pass away was Alice (seventeen) on 30 September 1802, and here the grim truth was revealed:

> A Consumption deep
> Laid us asleep,
> My sisters and I,
> Dear friends weep not in vain,
> But hope its for our Gain,
> That so soon did die.

In addition, two infant brothers and sisters were buried close by.

There were also a great number of 'afflictions' that could have been consumption or some other long-lasting and painful physical condition:

- 'Affliction sore long time I bore,/Physicians skill were vain,/Till Christ the chief gave me relief,/And eased me of my pain.' (Edward Preston, sixty-eight, Bulwick, January 1823)
- 'Affliction deep laid me asleep,/In death's cold shades I lie,/Grieve not my friends,/God makes amends,/Though I so young did die.' (Elizabeth Grimley, twenty-six, 1784)
- 'Our flesh afflicted was with pain,/Our bodies sore distrest,/Our souls to God we gave again,/To find eternal rest.' (Naseby)

At Sibbertoft, a fallen headstone marks the burial place of Sarah Ann Williams, twenty-four, a nurse and the daughter of a village shoemaker. Her unexpected death from tubercular peritonitis in February that year led to the inscription 'From pain forever free' appearing on the headstone. As a fitting tribute she was buried in her wedding dress. Tragedy struck the family once again when one of her brothers, William, a gamekeeper, committed suicide by shooting himself; he is also buried – in an unmarked spot – in the same churchyard.

The premature death of a father may have been due to some form of affliction. The following two inscriptions have almost identical verses:

- 'My years on earth, they were but few,/They wasted like the morning dew,/When I could stay no longer here,/I left my wife and children dear,/To the protection of kind Heaven,/When dying I hope to be forgiven.' (John Preston of Bulwick, thirty-three, 23 September 1818)
- 'My days on earth they were but few,/They wasted like the morning dew,/When I could stay no longer here,/I left my wife and babes so dear,/To the protection of kind heav'n,/And died in hope of being forgiven.' (William Perrin of Naseby, thirty-six, 21 January 1838)

The grave of Thomas Rye of Irthlingborough (*d.* 1795) has an element of caution in the inscription:

> Farewell, dear Wife and children all,
> For I must die, tho' you are small,
> O Serve the Lord, obey your Mother,
> You'll follow me, one time or other.

Whatever the cause of death, there is an element of hope and expectation of a better life to come after the body has suffered undignified treatment beneath the earth. The headstone of Ann Dunmore, who died at the age of thirty-seven at Rothwell in 1768, proclaims:

> The greedy worms devour my skin,
> And gnaw my wasting flesh,
> When God will build my Bones again,
> He clothes them all afresh.

Even earlier, the altar tomb of Elizabeth Buswell (*d.* 1636) at Clipston has a brass inscribed:

> See heere a cabinet, whose lem is gone,
> To fetch more lustre of Perfection,
> She was one heere yet wearie to remaine,
> Left here a Pledge for hir returne againe;
> And when her Saviours Glorie shall appeare,
> To give her light to fetch hir bodie here;

So may expect hir mongst celestiail Sprights,
Whose glorie shall ecclips all other lights,
Though gainst ye bodie wormes and tim come
Both shall together in the glory shine.

CHILDBIRTH

So many of the deaths of young women were the result of giving birth, often from complications arising from puerperal fever, a uterine infection and form of septicaemia caused by poor hygiene spread by a midwife or neighbour (or, in the case of the more affluent, by a physician). The problem was rife as late as the last decade of the nineteenth century. A look through any parish registers or at any funerary monument will reveal the horrifying statistics. A typical example of such an occurrence can be seen in the burials for Nassington in 1614–15, when a mother and child succumbed together:

> Joane Burton was buried the 7th of Februarie by moone light about two a clock in the morning, dying in childebed & not trimmed.

At Cottesbrooke: Sarah Sherman, aged thirty-six, 'dyd in child bed May ye 16 1751'. In the same village in October 1802, Ann Johnson, aged twenty-three, died in a similar manner, followed by her ten-month-old son, John, in March the following year.

One of the most poignant inscriptions in the county can be found in the churchyard at Maidwell, where a young mother succumbed, leaving her newborn baby of the same name, Lucy, with the father. He must have been particularly valued by his employer, who probably provided a headstone engraved with this elaborate verse, seemingly composed by a person with a degree of literacy:

> Here Lyeth the Body of Lucy, the Wife of Robert Tebbot, sometime gardener at this Hall, who dyed in Child Bed the 3 November Ano Dmi 1689, Aged 27 Yeares and 4 Moneths.
>
> Unhappy that nothing but thy Death,
> Would sorely turn to give thy infant breath,
> A stroke severe yet in it Heaven prove kind,
> A Lucy tooke, A Lucy left behind.

Visitors to the church of All Saints at Laxton may be surprised to see a marble wall tablet with the cryptic words: 'Ah, Julia!' and a nearby ledger inscribed in Latin, translated as:

> Ah Julia, most loving and beloved wife, most faithful of friends, most agreeable and kindly of women, Farewell. She died December 1760, aged 26.

A seventeenth-century headstone with a poignant verse dedicated to Lucy Tebbutt, who died during childbirth at Maidwell.

She was the wife of George Carbery, lord of the manor, who subsequently remarried. He died at the age of fifty in 1783.

At Northampton St Giles, the grieving husband of Ann Stonehouse, who died in 1747 at the age of twenty-five, shortly after the birth of her fourth child, had the following inscription added to her wall tablet:

> How lov'd and valu'd once avail'd thee,
> To whom related or by whom begot,
> A heap of Dust alone remains of Thee,
> 'Tis all Thou art, and all the Proud shall be.

Other notable inscriptions include that on a brass to Elizabeth Grant of Benefield, 1608:

> My Child-Bed was my Death Bed: thankes I gave,
> To God that gave a Child, and so I died.
> My body is entered in this Grave,
> My soule for which it long'd to Heaven her hied.
> My good-report they can record that knewe mee,
> A maide, a wife, a mother, then death slewe mee.

Another brass, at Barton Seagrave, was to Jane Floyde, 1616, inscribed:

Here she was borne and bred, here she was married, here did she live and dye, thus was she buried. This brass can say no more.

INFANT AND CHILD MORTALITY

> The silvery moon may wither in her prime,
> The golden sun itself will yield to time,
> The stars will dim but Chastity and Truth,
> Shall ever flourish in immortal Youth.
>
> (Wall tablet of Cassandra Whitley
> of Stamford St John, *d.* 1769)

Like many mothers who died giving birth, the survival rate of children was low. At Syresham an alabaster wall tablet (1718) in the chancel records the deaths in Latin of the five 'sleeping' sons of Robert Style, all of whom died within nine years of each other: Jacob in 1701, Jacob II in 1703, Henry in 1703, William in 1710. The fifth died elsewhere. (Another son, the eldest, survived and became the vicar of All Saints at Little Billing.) The inscription to Jeremiah Bates of Sibbertoft, three years old (*d.* October 1811) reads:

> Rest sweet babe! In gentle slumbers,
> Till the resurrection morn,
> Then arise to meet the numbers.
> That its triumph shall adorn,
> Tho' thy presence so endearing,
> We thy absence now deplore,
> At the saviour's bright appearing,
> We may meet ...

Parents could lose virtually all their children prematurely. Between 1817 and 1837, the Stiles family at Rushton lost no fewer than eight, all before the age of sixteen: John (fourteen) in 1807; William (also fourteen) in 1811; Mathilda (ten months) in 1817; Joseph (sixteen) in 1821; Mary Ann (fourteen) in 1823; and three others in infancy. Another son, Charles, managed to reach twenty-one (*d.* 1852).

The Clarke family at Kingscliffe lost seven daughters in succession: Emily Ann (eight months) in 1871; Sarah Ann (two years) in 1881; Kate (eleven) in 1884; Grace Cecilia (four) in 1888; Sarah Jane (two) in 1888; Fanny (sixteen) in 1891; and Louisa Anne (twenty-two) in February 1894. In the same village, the Philips family lost: Martha (eight) in 1845; William (twenty) in 1863; Rebecca (twenty-two) in 1863; Elizabeth (fifteen) in 1864; Alice (twenty-four) in 1877; and four children in infancy. The neighbouring Amos family lost: Sarah (twenty) in 1851; Josiah (fourteen) in 1853; Calvin (twenty) in 1854; Elizabeth (thirteen) in 1854; and five infants.

Some funerary inscriptions added extended poetic lines describing the parents' loss and grief, as was the case with nineteen-year-old Mary Thomas, the eldest daughter of Thomas and Elizabeth Bates. Mary died in August 1823:

> And art thou gone blest spirit, art thou gone,
> Or do I only dream! Oh no! Thou'rt gone,
> Gone to that nobler, brighter, happier world!
> Ah why, so early gain the peaceful shores,
> Of immortality and joy and love,
> Like blossom'd tress o'erturned by vernal storm,
> Lovely in death and beauteous ruin lay,
> And if in death still lovely, lovelier there, far lovelier.

A similar example can be found on a wall tablet inside the south porch of the church at Kingscliffe to Elizabeth Carrington, who died at the age of nineteen in March 1798:

> Think of her fate, revere the holy hand,
> That led her hence soon by steps,
> Long at her couch, Death to his patient stand,
> And menaced oft and oft withheld the blow,
> Then weep not Parents on her silent Grave,
> Her heav'n born Spirit with seraphic flight,
> Too pure to linger in its earthy cave,
> Wing's its free passage to the realms of light.

At Naseby is another poetic epitaph, albeit with a cautionary element, to an eight-year old, John Haddon (*d.* November 1738):

> I was a flower in my bud,
> Cropt off by death as God thought good,
> And you that read it shortly must,
> As well as I be laid in dust.

However, another inscription at Naseby, to Jacob Cheney, aged sixteen months (*d.* 30 August 1781), is of a more stark nature and reads:

> Dim miniature of greatness absolute,
> An heir of glory: A frail child of dust,
> Helpless Immortal: Insect infinite, A worm.

A wall tablet in the church at Blatherwycke records the death in 1858 of eleven-year-old Henry Stafford O'Brien:

A headstone in the churchyard of St Martin at Welton recording a local tragedy during the winter of 1806.

In Memory of a Beloved Child suddenly removed while at School by an Attack of Measles, from the Midst of his deeply sorrowing Family.

At Sulgrave, there are three interesting funerary floor lozenges that have to be interpreted by taking into account the differences between the old-style calendar (pre-September 1752) and the present-day calendar, which was instituted at the same time, when 1 January replaced 25 March (Lady Day) as the beginning of the New Year. Adjustments have to be made, therefore, with days between those two dates. The inscriptions on the lozenges commemorate the short lives of three daughters of the vicar, John Loggin, and his wife Sarah. Each daughter was christened Sarah in a futile attempt to have a girl with the mother's name, all of them dying before the age of five months: Sarah (13 November 1729–9 March 1729, i.e. 1730), Sarah (9 October 1729–1 March 1730/31), Sarah (b. 13 September 1732, died the same day).

At Ashley there is a cryptic inscription on the headstone of John Kirby, who died at the age of sixteen on 27 January 1832. One wonders if religious fanaticism was behind the wording, or if the son was vulnerable during his short life to undesirable influences in the neighbourhood:

> Yea, speedily was he taken away, Lest that wickedness should alter his understanding or deceit beguile his soul, for his soul pleased the Lord, therefore hasted he to take him away from all the wicked.

One of the most tragic inscriptions can be found on a headstone in the churchyard of St Martin at Welton that overlooks the street. It was erected by villagers, who had found a child in the vicinity on a cold winter's day, seemingly abandoned by his parents. It is inscribed:

> John, son of Peter and Eliz. Hewitt of Rugby. He was lost (by neglect), Jan 16, 1806 in a field in this parish & was found on the 18th starv'd to Death in the 6th year of his Age.

A white pillar memorial in the churchyard at Great Oakley records the deaths of George Pain, with his sister, mother and father (the latter couple founded the Particular Baptist Chapel at Wadcroft in Kettering). One cold January day in 1865, he was working at the windmill with his father when he was suddenly taken ill. He died a few days later, and his grief-stricken father subsequently left the boy's coat hanging on the inside of the door of the mill, never removing it during the remaining years of his working life. The mill was eventually demolished in 1895.

ACCIDENTS AND TRAGEDIES

Premature deaths, many of them from fire and falls, were commonplace, often at a relatively young age, although not all 'long' lives ran their natural course. A Great Oakley farmer, William Coales, aged eighty-nine, fell down the stairs of his house four years after his younger brother, Francis, had been thrown from a hay cart and killed. At Barton Seagrave in the nineteenth century, 107-year-old Gabriel Tudor fell into a fire and called out for help, but as there was no one around, he consequently perished. The parish registers recorded 'a sudden unnatural end for someone at such an age'.

One of the earliest recorded tragedies in the county was that included in the parish registers of Hemington for 1568. It refers to a group of men staying at the Hall: 'Francis Cooke was buried ye xijth of March 1568, John Timbowson, Thomas Gange, Thomas Werrington, William Skinner, were buried ye same day. All these five were killed with a dampe in one night in a newe lodging at the haule.'

The parish registers of Blakesley for 1601 refer to 'Richard Tomason falling out of a tree as he was gathering ivie on the Lordes day, tooke his death wound and was buried xxij, month of December.'

In the churchyard of All Saints at Rushton, a metal cross marks the burial place of George Jackson, who died in August 1897, and is inscribed: 'In affectionate remembrance of George, beloved son of Thomas and Fanny Jackson, accidentally killed, August 4th 1897, aged 12 years. Boast not thyself of tomorrow.' The parish magazine later gave further details, stating that he had been helping his father, who looked after the steam threshing machines on a farm. While at work, he was knocked down by a horse he was driving, 'and the wheel of the wagon passed over his neck and broke it. We believe he was spared any suffering, but it was an awful sudden call into the presence of his God.'

On the north side of the churchyard of St James at Paulerspury, a headstone inscription records the death of Richard Andrews, who was killed aged seventeen on 23 December 1840 by the Greyhound stagecoach, which regularly passed through the village on its route to and from Northampton. It was cold and slippery that particular day and, misjudging the conditions, he fell under the wheels of the moving coach and was killed instantly.

At Sudborough, a headstone on the south side of the churchyard of All Saints records how John Thomas was 'struck in the eye with a fork on the 8th July and died on the 10th, 1857, Aged 12 Years 9 Months'.

More silent is the inscription on the headstone of Samuel Harding, twenty, who was buried on the north side of the churchyard of All Saints at Wilbarston, and has this simple wording: 'This stone was erected in affectionate memory by his companions and friends.' The hidden story reveals how death can occur in the most innocuous of circumstances. It happened during the Stoke Albany Feast in June 1890, part of which was a cricket match between the village and neighbouring Wilbarston. While playing, he was hit on the head by a ball and died from the blow.

On 21 August 1884, Fanny Blaydes, wife of the rector of the church of St John the Baptist at Harringworth, was returning back to the village with two companions in a pony-drawn phaeton after visiting friends in Gretton. On the descent down a hill towards the village, the harness became loose and the shafts of the carriage suddenly rose up to the head of the pony, whereupon it panicked and galloped fast for about forty yards before colliding with some railings. In the confusion, Mrs Blaydes' companions had not noticed her disappearance. They subsequently got out of the carriage and ran back up the hill and found that she had been thrown from the carriage and was lying unconscious, seriously injured, on the grass verge. She was taken to the vicarage where a doctor was summoned, who examined her and found that her neck had been dislocated. She was later buried in the churchyard, but a stone memorial was erected at the spot she was found (still visible today in winter), inscribed: 'Hic Obit, F. M. B., Aug 21, 1884, Sudden Death, Sudden Glory.'

Careless shooting accidents were a fairly common occurrence. The headstone of John York at Deene (*d.* 1752) records that he was 'shot by accident, With gun and femur saltire-wise'. At Blatherwycke, there is a stone with a similar story: 'Martin Blades, son of Original and Elizabeth Blades died 25 years, 1844, who was killed near this spot by the accident of a gun.' Sometimes such an accident was recorded in other, less obvious, places. Francis Coales, a prosperous yeoman farmer at Aldwincle, wrote in his day book about the death of one of his young relatives: 'the above poor boy John Allen Coales met with a sad accident this day, July the fourth 1863. He was scaring

A page of Francis Coales's journal, recording the accidental death of a young relative.

crows away from some potatoes growing at the 2nd gates, and was laying or hanging the gun on the branches of an Ash.'

One of the most unusual premature deaths in the county must have been that of Eliza Gardner, wife of the curate of the church of St Lawrence at Long Buckby, where a wall tablet records her demise. They were woken up late one night in July 1840 by the sound of someone breaking into their home. The curate went to investigate while Eliza remained in bed. The drunken intruders were later caught, but the occurrence had a knock-on effect. Believed to have been in a fragile state of health at the time, the incident had exacerbated her condition. She had immediately died of shock.

A series of uncanny occurrences occurred at Culworth, beginning in the seventeenth century, all of which involved one of the church bells. According to the parish registers, Edward Elder was killed 'upon Tuesday in Easter Week' in 1694 by the bell falling on him. It fell again twice more *on the same day of the same month*, without causing death, although on one of these occasions, in April 1863, the parish clerk had a narrow escape when the bell just missed him. Just as uncanny were the deaths of Joseph Pope of Clipston in 1803 and his brother the following year, at the same place and in the same manner. Both were run over by a horse and carriage at the corner of a road. Joseph had had his leg broken on the same spot the week before his death.

The parish registers for Deene in 1724 record the death of two men repairing the north aisle of the church. The roof collapsed on them: 'Charity Harrison, a Deenethorpe labourer and a Weldon man, Robert Richardson, died of a mortification occasioned by the fall of the Church.'

With the arrival of the railway in Northamptonshire during the nineteenth century, it was inevitable that the work involved would lead to casualties. While the Kettering-to-Manton line of the Midland Railway was being laid, there were at least two deaths. At Great Oakley, the inscription on the headstone of one labourer thinly veils the cause of death: 'Remembrance of James Edwards, a navvy, son of Edward Edwards of Becken Hollow, Somersetshire, who died suddenly on the 25th June 1876, aged 40 years.' At neighbouring Little Oakley, the inscription was more forthcoming: 'In Memory of William Thomas Winfield, who was killed on the Kettering to Manton Railway in the course of construction, October 8, 1877. Aged 29 years.'

MURDERS

> It was C——s B——w that brought me to an end,
> Dear parents mourn not for me, for God will stand my friend.
> With half a Pint of Poyson, He came to visit me,
> Write this on my Grave, That all who read may see.
>
> (Headstone inscription at Wolstanton, 1763)

Murders have always been commonplace, and Northamptonshire is no exception. On a badly eroded headstone adjacent to the church tower at Laxton, the cause of death of Thomas Milley in 1687 was recorded as 'killed by gypsies the 13 May, 1[6]87, in the — year of his age.' A group of gypsies camping nearby had been drinking on his premises and refused to pay up, whereupon the leader's wife stabbed him to death.

In July 1855, Benjamin Cheney, an eighty-one-year-old Rothwell farmer and miller, was making his way to the market in Kettering with a large amount of silver and copper coins in his pockets. At 'the fourth stile', he was attacked by nineteen-year-old Isaac Pinnock with an axe and was instantly killed. He was found by local folk with a 4-inch gash 'cutting into his brain'. Witnesses had seen the accused leaving the scene, walking in his usual awkward manner (being semi-paralysed). The money was found on him, and his father later testified to the axe having gone missing at the time – it was found close to the scene of the crime. Pinnock was found guilty and sentenced to death, but this was subsequently commuted to imprisonment in Broadmoor, where he died thirty-two years later. The inscription on the headstone of the victim on the south side of the church has the inscription, 'Fear not them which kill the body,/But are not able to kill the soul.'

When Louisa Johnson was visiting her sister in Finedon, her spurned lover followed her, and, during a heated argument while they were walking together, he slit her throat. The metal gravemarker at Burton Latimer, where she was buried, records:

In affectionate remembrance of Louisa Sophia Johnson of Cranfield, Beds. Died Feb 8th 1893 aged 29 years. 'He brought down my strength in my journey and shortened my days.'

CAUTIONARY VERSE

> Thy beauty shall no more be found,
> Nor in thy marble vault shall sound
> My echoing song: then worms shall try
> That long preserved virginity,
> And your quaint honour turned to dust,
> And into ashes all my lust.
> The grave's a fine and private place,
> But none I think do there embrace.'
>
> (Andrew Marvell, 'To His Coy Mistress')

The popular and spectacular medieval play *Dance of Death* (see Chapter 6) included these lines: 'Man behold so as I am now, so shalt thou be,/Gold and silver shall make no plea,/This daunce to defend, but follow me.' It fired the public imagination for centuries and led to a spate of similar cautionary lines appearing on funerary monuments. There are many examples around the county, a few of which are listed here, all of which remind the passer-by of the transience of life and the inevitability of death for everyone.

An inscription at Welton (1699) reads, 'Stay, Reader, shed a teare,/On this just man that slumbereth here./And whilst thou readest thus on me,/Think of the glass that runs for thee.'

On a brass to Samuel Wyman, Kingscliffe (*d.* 1700): 'Know, Reader, that in dust I lie,/That as you are, so once was I,/And as I am, so must you be,/Therefore prepare to follow me.'

On a chest tomb in the churchyard at Wadenhoe: 'Sarah, the wife of Edward Holditch departed this life April the 2nd 1729, Age 65. Reeder art thou in Health,/So ware I./But fore days Before, I was to die./Short was my life,/The longer my rest,/God takes them soonest/Whom he lovest best./So here I leave thee,/All wee come to see the day of Christ and there see thee.'

On a wall tablet inside the porch of the church of St Peter at Oundle: 'Beneath Lies Eleanor, wife of Edward Raymond who died Fbrey 20, 1744, In ye 45 year of her Age. Also six children who Died in their Infancy. Reader, consider that thou also art but Dust.'

Other cautionary inscriptions show that although death comes to everyone, it can happen when least expected. At Clipston, the headstone of John Sharman (*d.* 1788) reads, 'Who ere thou art, readst this stone,/Consider that soon I was fine,/At night in perfect health was I,/Next morning in Eternity./Then flee to Christ, make no delay,/For no-one knows their dying day.'

At Cottesbrooke, Esther Holt (*d.* May 1865, aged twenty-eight): 'A sudden change, I in a short time fell./And had not time to bid my friends farewell,/Think nothing strange, death happens unto all./My lot's today, tomorrow you may fall.'

At Pytchley the headstone of sixteen-year-old Clementina Honor Gue (*d.* November 1832) reads, 'Seize Mortals! Seize the Present Hour,/Improve each moment as it flies,/Life's a short summer, Man a flower,/He dies, Alas! How soon he dies.'

At Marston Trussell, Elizabeth Sprigg (*d.* June 1775, aged thirty-five): 'Beneath this stone concealed from human eyes,/The mouldering relics of a maiden lies,/Reader prepare, reflect whilst this you view,/Who next may die, uncertain – why not you.'

Mary Andrews (*d.* 1861) in the churchyard at Blatherwycke: 'As falls the leaves neath Autumn's withering blast,/So die mankind, their spring and summer past,/Yes thou ere long must lie neath the sod,/Then young and old prepare to meet thy God.'

Sometimes cautionary inscriptions could contain a reminder to the living of their need to perform necessary duties, such as that of Robert Sanderson (*d.* 1674) at Wadenhoe: 'With him that lyes here nere trouble thy head,/remember the old saying speake well of the dead.' At Naseby, a similar caution is given on the headstone of Robert Henson (*d.* 1742): 'Farewell vain world, Bid adue [*sic*] to thee,/I value not what thou canst say of me,/Thy smiles I crave not nor thy frowne I fear,/Alais for me, my head lies quiet here./What thou hast seen amis in me, Take care and shun,/And look at home [w]here is something to be done.' An adamant request can be found at Desborough on the headstone of Ann Yeomans (*d.* 1832): 'It was my mind for to lie here,/Move not my bones till Christ appear.'

More ominous was that of another headstone which was erected in the churchyard at Bozeat, for John and Mary Partridge in 1840, during an era when the practice of bodysnatching for scientific research was taking place: 'May all the afflictions of Job be the lot that disturbs the remains of those that repose below.'

WARS AND ACTIVE SERVICE

No one needs reminding of the devastation that war can cause. Among the most unfortunate families were the Tryons of Bulwick, who lost several members on active service. All around Bulwick church are wall tablets and stained-glass windows erected in memory of the lost Tryons, the most ornate being a wall monument to Vice Admiral Sir George Tryon, who died with 300 of his men when his ship, HMS *Victoria*, collided with HMS *Camperdown* during manoeuvres in the Mediterranean and sank off the coast of Beirut in 1893. The memorial includes a bust of the deceased.

Beneath a tree, west of the porch of the church at Naseby, a slate headstone inscription reads:

> In memory of Edward Perkins, serjeant in the 23rd regiment of the Royal Welch Fusiliers at Minorca, when taken, and five battles in Germany who being worn out with 16 years service, departed this life May 9th 1767 in the 40th year of his age. Bravely didst thou serve thy King and Country.

A wall tablet in the chancel of the church at Easton on the Hill is dedicated to members of the Skynner family, one of whom was the rector for forty-two years. Among the other names is that of his son John, a naval post-captain who drowned when his frigate, *La Lutine*, was wrecked off the coast of Holland in October 1799. He was thirty-three. The bell of the ship was salvaged by the insurers, Lloyd's, and is still used today to alert underwriters of any urgent matter. A commemorative plaque is affixed to the boundary wall of the old rectory (Lutine House) in the village.

There are mysteries surrounding some wartime burials. One example is at Weldon, where a German Dornier bomber was shot down in February 1943. The five-man crew was killed outright and they were subsequently buried in the village churchyard in a common grave covered with a German flag in front of a large gathering. Initially only one grave marker had a name – that of the captain. The others bore just a cross with the words 'An unknown German airman'. Afterwards the names were added, except for one, which stayed as it was. In 1963, the remains of the crew were disinterred with due ceremony and buried at the German Military Cemetery at Cannock Chase, where they still lie. But speculation was rife; the identity of the fifth person has never been satisfactorily explained. Dornier aircraft normally had a four-man crew and this one was flying low at 6,000 feet, so the most likely solution is that he was one of a number of spies being parachuted into the county at the time. At the time there was a strategically important steel works nearby.

LONGEVITY

Considering that the average life span for people until the early eighteenth century was forty for men and forty-five for women, it was exceptional if an individual could reach his or her hundredth year. Job Orton, first warden at Latham's Hospital, Barnwell St Andrew, died in 1607 aged 101. At Milton Malsor in 1601, Maud Dunkley was 'buried ye 23rd of February, Anno aetatis, suae' (i.e. in the hundredth year of her age). At Cransley, a wall tablet in the nave records, 'Near this place lieth inter'd the Body of Samuel Willis, born in this Parish, he died March the First in the year 1753 in the 100th year of his age.'

Other centenarians include the aptly named Alice Old at Weedon Bec, who lived through six different 'reigns' from Charles I to Queen Anne, while a brass under the carpet in the nave of the church of St John the Baptist at Harringworth commemorates Matthew Palmer, a former vicar who died in 1752 at the age of 110. But it is two members of the Bailes family in Northampton that can claim to have held the record for longevity in the county, *if claims were correct*. James Bailes is said to have lived frugally on brown bread, cheese, water and small beer, his sight failing at 124 years old and his death occurring four years later. A relative, John Bailes, died in April 1706, his epitaph reading, 'Hereunder lyeth John Bailes, born in this town. He was above 126 years old and had his health, sight and memory to ye last. He lived in three centuries and was buried ye 14th April, 1706.'

Old Scarlett, who was a sexton at Peterborough, died at the age of ninety-eight in July 1594, and was renowned for having buried two queens (Catherine of Aragon and Mary, Queen of Scots) and for having lived 'twice over his life's space', during which time he had dug graves for all his relatives and several successive owners of the house he lived in. He had long prepared his own grave, but because he carried on living to an amazingly old age (for the time), it was thought he would never use it. A large painting

A depiction of the renowned sixteenth-century Peterborough sexton Old Scarlett.

of him, with the following verse, may be seen on a wall at the rear of the cathedral, close to the entrance:

> You see Old Scarlett's Picture standing on hie,
> But at your Feete, doth his Body lye.
> His gravestone doth his Age and Death time show,
> His office by theis Tokens you may know.
> Second to none for Strength and sturdye Limm,
> A scababe mighty Voice, hath Visage grim.
> Hee had two Queenes within this Place,
> And this Towne's Householders, his live's Space.
> Twice over, but at length, his own Turne came,
> What hee for others did for him the same was done:
> No doubt his Soule doth live for aye
> In Heaven, though here his Body be clad in Clay.

Sometimes a little humour could creep into a funeral. John Clifton, the Oundle carpenter and workhouse overseer, wrote in his diary in 1810, 'Old Mrs Clark of Astwell was buried tonight. She had her Grave Stone set down many years ago, but could not quite manage the Task. Aged 90.'

OCCUPATIONAL

A unique group of headstone inscriptions reflect the crafts and trades that the members of the community had been engaged in during their lives. Gardeners seem to have been held in particularly high regard by their employers, as can be seen in churchyards such as those at Maidwell and Potterspury, where there is an unusually elaborate wall monument to John Mead (*d.* 1742), gardener to the Duke of Grafton at Wakefield Lodge. At Wicken, the inscription to John Jackson, who died in 1785, is particularly poetic:

> This man he was a gardener by trade,
> His work was chiefly using the spade,
> At Wicken Park he earned his daily bread,
> Raking the ground whereon he used to tread,
> The rake's laid by, together with his spade,
> His scythe hung up, and trowl put in the shade,
> His seeds are sown, his line is now wound up,
> His trees are pruned, his knife is also shut,
> His hoe is left, likewise his shears,
> And here he sleeps in peace free from all cares.

At Great Oakley, various members of the manorial de Capell Brooke family seem to have placed great value on the services of certain employees. The first was the explorer Sir Arthur de Capell Brooke (1791–1858), who was absent from Great Oakley Hall for much of the time and relied on the honesty and diligence of his servants, one of whom died relatively young. In gratitude for his services, de Capell Brooke provided a headstone inscribed:

> In memory of Henry Griffin of Sibbertoft in this county who after a short but severe illness, exchanged this life for immortality July 1829 in the 38th year of his age. He lived respected and esteemed and died regretted by the family in which he has been for many years and this stone was placed over his grave by his master, Arthur de Capel Brooke esq. in remembrance of a good and faithful servant.

Forty-six years later, another member of the family, Captain Arthur Watson de Capell Brooke – who had been staying at Great Oakley Hall for a number of years while the manorial family was living in another of its homes at Market Harborough – had a headstone erected for another employee, inscribed: 'John Dawkins, 68, died July 1875 for 45 years a gardener of Great Oakley Hall … in affectionate remembrance of his faithful services.' The tradition was continued by the barrister Sir William de Capell Brooke, who rebuilt much of the village (and added a school for the community) between 1858 and 1872. The new headstone was dedicated to 'John Patrick for 48 years, gamekeeper at Great Oakley who died January 24th 1878 aged 77 years. This stone was erected by Sir William de Capell Brooke, Bart, in affectionate remembrance of his long and faithful service.'

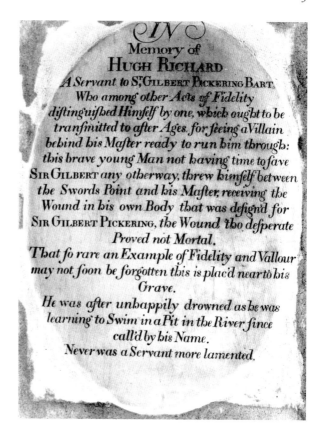

The ironic inscription on a wall tablet of a dedicated servant of Sir Gilbert Pickering of Titchmarsh.

An ornate elliptical wall tablet in the church of St Andrew in Brigstock was erected by Lord and Lady Lyveden in 1867 to Elizabeth Knox, their 'Worthy, Trustful Housekeeper for Twenty Years'.

One particular servant, however, showed outstanding bravery and lack of concern for his own life while in the service of his master at Titchmarsh, with a twist of irony sealing his fate:

> In Memory of Hugh Richard, a Servant to Sir Gilbert Pickering, Bart, Who Among other Acts of Fidelity distinguished Himself by one, which ought to be transmitted to after Ages, for seeing a Villain behind his Master ready to run him through, this brave young Man not having time to save Sir Gilbert any other way, threw himself between the Swords Point and his Master, receiving the Wound on his own Body, that was design'd for Sir Gilbert Pickering, the wound tho' desperate proved not mortal. That so rare an Example of Fidelity and Vallour may not soon be forgotten this is plac'd near to his Grave. He was after unhappily drowned as he was learning to swim in a pit in the river, since call'd by his Name. Never was a servant more lamented.

At All Saints in Northampton there was formerly a witty inscription to a cobbler who was known to enjoy a tipple or two during his lifetime:

> Close without the narrow stall,
> Lives one who was friend to awl,
> He save the soles from getting worse,
> But cursed his own without remorse,
> And though a drunken life he passed,
> He saved his sole by mending at the last.

A stock inscription to blacksmiths was once found all around England and there is at least one nineteenth-century example, at Weldon to John White:

> My sledge and hammer lie reclined,
> My bellows too have lost their wind.
> My fires extinct, my forge decayed,
> And in the dust my vice is laid.
> My coals are spent, my iron gone,
> My last nail struck, my work is done.

Stonemasons are also represented. In one particularly strange case at Laxton, there is a double-gabled chest tomb that has no names or dates, only a cryptic inscription: 'Near this Place lieth buried the generation of Masons.' At Yarwell, another family group, the Sandersons, are buried. One of them, William (*d.* 1803), has the following inscription:

> Tread lightly on his ashes
> ye men of genius,
> For he was your kinsman,
> Weed his grave clear
> ye men of goodness,
> For he was your brother,
> But alas, alas!
> He is gone, his genius fled,
> To the stars from whence it came,
> And that warm heart with all its
> Generous and open vessels are
> Comprised in a clod of the valley.

At Lowick there is a headstone to a local trader:

> Richard Taylor now to rest has gone,
> His dust remains near this inscripted stone,
> A quiet neighbour and a friend sincere,
> Beloved by all who his acquaintance were,
> An honest dealer, to the poor a friend,
> Was very fond of music to his latest end,

In April month on the fateful day,
The King of Terrors snatched his life away.

The police have also seen tragedy among their ranks, either in the course of carrying out their duties or otherwise. At Naseby, a headstone describes the death in 1878 of twenty-seven-year-old David Davies 'of Northamptonshire Constabulary, severely injured while in the discharge of his duty at Kettering'. At Rothwell, the headstone of a police sergeant, Isaac Wilson, records, 'He had been a member of the Force onwards of 11 years and his death was the result of a rail accident in Northampton on the night of 18 October 1877.'

PETS

As well as humans being commemorated, a number of pets were likewise given a special burial place and marker by their owners, with cats, dogs and horses being particularly valued during their lives. In 1777, the owner of a cat in Northampton marked its grave in his garden with the heading 'A Favourite Cat' and the following long epitaph:

The turf beneath this arching shade,
By beauty's tears is hallow'd made,
This dust was once alive as thou,
Think, thou shalt be, what is this now?
Could winning manners, loveliest form,
With nature's genuine feelings warm,
Could female softness, manly fire,
Could gratitude with these conspire,
To save a mortal form from his doom,
Remembrance might have spar'd this tomb,
Ask'st thou who sleeps beneath this stone?
One to the noisy world unknown,
One who, secure of dearer form,
Marks not the marble with her name.
Nor think the tear alone design'd,
To mourn the loss of human-kind,
The gentle maid who weeps her end,
Can in a cat lament a friend.

In the eighteenth century, two dogs belonging to the manorial O'Brien family were buried with small markers in the hall grounds at Blatherwycke, near the track to Kingscliffe, while in the grounds of Rushton Hall, in an area known as 'The Wilderness', the daughters of Viscount Cullen would bury their many pets, including cats, birds and two favourite dogs, the grave of the latter being marked with the inscription, 'Dido and Jack one fateful day,/Were mixed with their native clay.'

In 1734, at Easton Neston, a three-year-old dog, Pug, was buried in even more elaborate surroundings – in a 'temple' set within the hall grounds:

> No Balzon'd Coat or Sculptur'd Bone,
> Honours scarcely deem our own,
> Adorn this simple rustic Stone,
> But Love and Friendship without Blame.
> With Gratitude we justly claim;
> Not unlamented now she dies;
> Besprinkled here this Tribute lies,
> With heavenly Tears from Angel Eyes.

Similarly, at Kettering, an eight-year-old dog named Jerry, which had belonged to the entrepreneur Charles Wicksteed, was buried in 1928 in a sunken garden beneath the bandstand of the celebrated Wicksteed Park. The site was marked by a statue and plaque inscribed:

> Closely bound to a human heart,
> Little brown dog, You had your part,
> In the Levelling, Building, Staying of Stream,
> In the Park That Arose from your Master's Dreams.

Cotherstone, a prize-winning racehorse that won the 2,000 Guineas and the Derby in 1843, is buried at Harlestone, where there is a commemorative plaque set in a wall adjoining the sports field. At nearby Chapel Brampton, according to tradition, Merry Tom Lane is named after a favourite horse of Earl Spencer, which was used in the hunt but later died while jumping a brook in the vicinity. It is said to be buried with its saddle and bridle, and a stone was erected in its memory. At Bulwick, two horses were buried in a field and later disinterred and reburied outside the walls of the vicarage, the plots marked by headstones. Again at Rushton Hall, two celebrated steeplechase horses were buried under a mound in The Wilderness. An inscription on an accompanying stone on the mound reads:

> These two nags as people say,
> Do show the Pytchley gents the way,
> And on the 7th day called Sunday,
> Will go from church to church till Monday.

Not a pet but a quarry of the chase was commemorated on a stone tablet set in a wall adjoining the former maltings of the Elworthy Brewery at Kettering. It is still *in situ*, but with a faded inscription: 'Who Woop! This Stone Marks The Spot Where A Fox Was Found At Leggard's Copse. Was Killed By The Pytchley Hunt. January 14, 1907.'

6

IMAGES OF DEATH

Yet even these bones from insult to protect,
Some frail monument still erected nigh,
With uncouth rhymes and shapeless sculpture decked,
Implores the passing tribute of a sigh.
(Thomas Gray, 'Elegy Written in a Country Churchyard', 1751)

In the early medieval era, masons and woodcarvers had no pattern books of their own from which to draw inspiration and had to rely on figures from earlier stonework, illustrated manuscripts, and work in ivory, enamel and metal. Craftsmen who worked with the latter materials had long-established traditions and contacts with their counterparts in the Middle East and elsewhere; they also had contact with foreign traders, who brought patterned silks, ornaments and other works of art with exotic images and unusual motifs into the country. There was also the second-century *Physiologus*, a book describing natural and unnatural things – both animate and inanimate – that had appeared in earlier mythologies and the work of classical writers, or else had been discovered in Alexander the Great's vast empire. In addition, there were bestiaries, books illustrating a range of both common and strange creatures. They were considered to be an allegorical guide to the divine purpose of creation.

The crusades brought Europe into further contact with oriental styles and fashions. In the thirteenth century, a book of architectural notes and sketches appeared by Villard de Honnecourt, a French traveller who had visited churches and cathedrals all around Europe. This and subsequent pattern books set the trend for future masons and other craftsmen. The Renaissance, with its emphasis on mortality, brought in another stock of images, which led to seventeenth-century Baroque and the lighter, Rococo form of the early eighteenth century (including swags, festoons, scrolls, animal forms, mythological figures, shells, flowers, fruit, garlands and drapery). From the middle years of the eighteenth century, the Neoclassical style predominated, with, as the name implies, realistic portrayals of figures in Grecian or Roman costume, wreaths, palms, torches, urns and other classical features. That same century was an era of pattern books with a hitherto unprecedented range of images for funerary masons to show clients and to use in their work. One particularly popular book was Mathias Lock and Henry Copland's *A New Book of Ornaments* (1752).

During the Victorian period, however, individual craftsmanship disappeared as mass-produced memorials were advertised in run-of-the-mill, uninspiring 'catalogues' with stock images from which the growing population could choose according to price and means. Calligraphic lettering gave way to plainer and more deeply incised typographical lettering. At the same time, the influential religious Oxford (or Tractarian) Movement, a vigorous expression of Anglo-Catholicism, saw symbolism as having too many pre-Christian elements, and this tended to have a knock-on effect on funerary art, with headstone engraving becoming increasingly confined to simple motifs (like clasped hands, a plain cross, or foliage) and funerary inscriptions. This chapter explores some of the more common and interesting images before the Victorian 'decline'.

EARLY CHURCHYARD MEMORIALS

Before the closing years of the sixteenth century, churchyard graves were either unmarked or had a wooden post (or similar marker), all of which have long since perished. Thereafter, more permanent headstones came into being throughout the seventeenth century, gradually gaining popularity among those who could afford them. At first small and crudely inscribed with a name and date of death, they were occasionally accompanied by a simple image, commonly a skull, bones, or both, symbolising the one thing certain in life – death. An example is the skull and crossbones image at Helmdon (1675). A similar situation occurred inside the church with ledgers, a good example of which can be seen in the south aisle of the church of St John the Baptist at Corby, dedicated to John Lee (*d*. 1652). This image is discussed in more detail below.

A typical small seventeenth-century headstone with skull and crude inscription at Great Oakley.

Flowers have always been noted for their beauty, their colour and their association with the earth from which they spring. They have consequently been placed on graves for centuries, as a sign of remembrance and respect. It is no wonder that these traits were reflected in a great many names that were traditionally given to girls, such as Rose, Lily, May, Violet, Primrose, Daisy, Heather, Iris and Ivy. Less common were tree names like Rowan, Ash and Holly.

Trees were anciently regarded as sacred entities, linking the world beneath our feet, the world we live in, and the 'world' above our heads. They were seen as symbols of longevity or immortality, lasting several human lifetimes. There are ash and beech trees surviving today in the county at Fineshade and Wakerley woods that were planted in the earlier years of the seventeenth century. Some oaks, no longer with us, lived to a great age, attaining immense girths and height in the process. Other trees could live even longer, notably the yew, which regenerates from within when the core of the tree dies. This is *one* of the reasons why the yew can be seen in churchyards; another is that many were planted by order of Edward I to give shelter to the fabric of the church building from the elements, in particular protection against south-westerly gales, but also against evil influences. The best examples are at Stoke Albany, Marston St Lawrence, Croughton, Helmdon and Thorpe Mandeville. A number also appeared in the county when the new Diocese of Peterborough was created in 1541, replacing the Diocese of Lincoln, which had favoured the sallow.

Not surprisingly, some flowers, trees and plants would have had symbolic importance. Those connected with death were the pansy (remembrance), poppy (sleep), lily (resurrection), willow (mourning) and olive branch (peace). Carnations were said to have sprung from the graves of lovers. Evergreens like the laurel, seeming never to die, were seen as a symbol of immortality. Rosemary, depending on the occasion or mourner, could symbolise remembrance, fidelity or immortality. Buds were equated with new life, while ears or sheaves of wheat symbolised the body of Christ and his resurrection.

Even a surname with roots in the natural world could be considered imbued with symbolism. This was used to great effect on the 'foliate' headstone inscription of Marie Hart, née Green, of Dallington, asserting her return to her maiden status in her 'new life':

> July ye 30, 1647,
> Since when in part,
> Here lieth Marie Hart,
> Hath fading lien,
> Who was before,
> And wil much more,
> Be Marie Green.

Thus flower, plant and tree images would often be engraved on headstones and wall memorials, sometimes sumptuously, as on a sixteenth-century wall monument at Nether Heyford, an eighteenth-century headstone at Syresham, and a thirteenth-century coffin lid at Gayton. Other examples might reflect the sadness of an untimely death, such as that on a headstone close to the porch of the church of All Saints at Laxton, which shows a broken flower with what seems to be a face bearing an expression of grief. There might also be a 'sympathetic' background echoing a widow's grief, where the overhanging branch, which forms an arc over the head of the female figure, has snapped into two places – as can be seen at Aldwincle All Saints and Titchmarsh. A similar effect was sometimes achieved with a rose. The motif is probably influenced by the Biblical book of Job – 'He cometh forth like a flower, and is cut down' (14:2).

Even the Green Man had a degree of involvement with some of the county's funerary monuments in his two traditional roles – to protect and to encourage life (in this case, resurrection). Although his image became more stylised – almost beyond recognition in some cases – after the Reformation, his function remained the same. The earliest depiction can be found in the Norman church of St Peter in Northampton, on a sumptuously carved twelfth-century coffin lid where the figure has a cornucopia of foliage, fruit and birds issuing from his mouth. He next appears with mouth foliage on a roof boss on the vaulted roof in the thirteenth-century crypt of the church of St Peter at Oundle. From the same century, he appears with a leaf emerging from each side of his mouth on the Easter sepulchre of the church of St Nicholas at Twywell. He is depicted on the base of the tomb of two fourteenth-century wooden effigies in the church of St James at Paulerspury, and beside the entrance to the chapel of Sir Henry de Vere at Great Addington (the church of All Saints). From the following century he appears on the Seymour tomb at St Mary's in Higham Ferrers, and on the tomb of Sir John Wydervyl at St Mary's, Grafton Regis. The Elizabethan era is represented by wall memorials to the York family at Fotheringhay, to Sir Thomas Griffin at Braybrooke, and to William and Elizabeth Markham at Little Oakley – the first two examples with sumptuous foliage and fruit. From the seventeenth century, he can be found on a tomb canopy at Thenford, and in the Jenison wall monument (1681) at Irchester. Thereafter, during the Enlightenment, he went out of fashion as a funerary feature in Northamptonshire.

SKULLS, SKELETONS AND SHROUDS

During the Renaissance, a number of popular motifs were used in funerary art: pilasters, strapwork, wreaths, allegorical figures, bow and arrows, spear, bell, snakes, the skull or death's head, spade, sundial, scythe, hourglass and skeleton. Of these, nothing so aptly portrays the image of death than the latter three motifs, personifying 'Death' or 'the Grim Reaper'.

During the thirteenth century, a French tale (translated into Middle English in the fifteenth century) appeared, called 'The Three Quick and the Three Dead' (i.e. 'The Three Living and the Three Dead'). It tells the story of three kings out hunting, during which time they get separated from their retainers in a mist. They then meet three skeletons, or corpses, who claim to be the kings' ancestors and chide them about their lives of pleasure. The reaction among the men varies from wanting to flee to one of confrontation. Later, however, they build a church with paintings depicting their encounter. The message is about the transience of life: 'always remember the dead' (something that fitted in well with the policy of doing good work to shorten one's time in Purgatory). There is a fine depiction of the encounter among a series of remarkably well-preserved wall paintings in the nave of the church of St Mary in Raunds, while there are fragments on another (fourteenth-century) wall painting in the church of St Leonard at Glapthorn.

At the same time, in the 1440s, another European image and concept, the *Danse Macabre* – which has its roots in the time of the Black Death, which had swept across Europe in the previous century – was translated into English by John Lydgate as the *Dance of Death*. It was subsequently painted on the walls of the cloisters and cemetery of the Pardonkirkhay, St Paul's (demolished in 1549), where it certainly struck a chord. There were further paintings and spectacular performances similar in nature to the mystery plays, in which Death would appear as the messenger of God, leading men in a slow dance to their new home. Figures in skeleton costume emerged from the grave to address and accompany representatives from all classes of society – princes and kings, religious leaders, rich and poor, young and old – usually twenty-four in number. The message was 'death comes to all, there is no escape, so be prepared'.

The following are just a few examples of where the images may be seen in churchyards around the county. At Piddington, one headstone is of special interest in not just depicting a skull, but a variety of other funerary images: thigh bone, trumpet, spade, 'live torch', hourglass, celestial crown and ouroborous (a serpent forming a circle by biting its tail – a symbol of eternity and eternal recurrence). At Towcester, a small headstone with a skull image can be found lying partially hidden beneath a bush close to the chancel. Skulls and crossbones can be found on a 1675 headstone at Helmdon; similarly at Great Oakley, on one of two small headstones to Roger Manton (*d.* 1681), son of the village carpenter, and his mother, Dorothy (*d.* 1682). By the porch at Easton on the Hill, an eighteenth-century headstone depicts a crown over the skull and crossbones, with attendant cherubs. On the outside wall of the manorial Palmer family chapel at the church of St Peter in East Carlton, a label stop on the east window has a skull overlooking the family vault. Embedded in the churchyard wall at Benefield is an eighteenth-century stone tablet with a well-carved skull staring out at the onlooker.

The images are also well represented inside a church. The skull with wings represented the soul ascending into heaven, and there are a number of examples, including one on the south wall of the chancel, where the image forms the base of a marble wall tablet to Susanna Robinson (1714) that also includes her own self-written epitaph. Similar large, winged skulls can be seen on an oval wall tablet at Culworth to Judith Rye (*d.* 1698), together with an urn and doves; on the base of a wall monument at Dodford; and another, with a crown, on the seventeenth-century black marble wall monument at Apethorpe, dedicated to Rowland Woodward.

Very effective but not necessarily common are hollow eyes in skull images, but there is a set of these at Stoke Doyle on the base of a hanging monument representing the children of Frances Palmer, who is depicted with her husband kneeling beside her (1628).

Between the broken pediments of the wall monument to Thomas Law (*d.* 1714) in the chancel of the church of All Saints and St James at Kingscliffe is a small flesh-coloured skull, combined with a thick worm and a leafy stem – a dramatic if unobtrusive way of representing death and resurrection.

A sinister-looking set of motifs can be seen on the altar tomb of Elizabeth Buswell (*d.* 1636) at Clipston, where the panels are decorated with a jumble of mortality images bound together with worm-like ribbons: a skull pierced with bones, spade, scythe, hourglass, open book and trumpets

Some monuments are very cleverly composed, such as that in front of the east window in the north chapel of the church of St Peter at Lowick, where the memorial to Lady Mordaunt (*d.* 1705) has a skull peeping out from under the cushion on which she is resting, with other symbols of mortality at each end of the tomb. At Whiston, a standing monument (1700) depicts a child holding a skull, and a baby in swaddling clothes. Even more startling are death's heads peering out from behind a curtain on a headstone at Orlingbury.

In the nave of the church of St John the Baptist at Harringworth there is a brass (now under carpet) to a former vicar, William Gardener (*d.* 1680), and his wife Elizabeth (*d.* 1719), with the engraving of a skull. Under the tower of the church of St John the Baptist at Achurch (but from the demolished church at nearby Lilford) is a wall tablet to Arthur Elmes (*d.* 1663), depicting a skull and bones.

The wall monument with banded obelisks of Ann Breton at Norton (*d.* 1635) depicts a wreathed skull in an open segmental pediment. The combination of a skull and foliage on the cartouche of a wall tablet at Greatworth (1741) symbolises victory over death and ultimate renewal.

Skeletal images are even more spectacular. One particularly imposing monument to Thomas Langton Freke (*d.* 1769) can be found at Kings Sutton; it shows triumph over death in the form of Christ trampling a skeleton. A brass at Church Brampton (1585) depicts a skeleton instead of a human figure, while at Ashby St Ledger there is a unique wall painting showing a skeleton holding a spade. In the south chapel of the church of St Andrew at Cransley, there is a very large skeleton engraved on an eroded floor slab (1557, now under the carpet for protection) to Edward and Anne Barnewell.

In additional to his skeletal form, Death was frequently depicted as an old man holding a scythe and hourglass. The image was probably based on the old Roman god Saturn. Inside Peterborough Cathedral is a sixteenth-century alabaster wall plaque depicting an elderly, benign-looking, almost-human, winged 'Death' holding an hourglass in his left hand and a scythe in the right. The handle rests on a skull and bones. In the church of St Michael at Great Oakley, he appears in younger form on a misericord. In the raised churchyard of St Mary at Titchmarsh, he appears on a great number of eighteenth-century headstones (some in excellent condition) east of the porch and north of the chancel, scythe in his right hand, and hourglass in his left, pouring sand over a 'portrait' medallion of the deceased.

Depictions of figures in shrouds are less common, but there have been interesting examples on brasses in the county that are no longer complete, having suffered theft or mutilation at some time in the past. At Ashby St Ledger, there is a damaged fifteenth-century brass to Sir William Catesby and his wife, one of whom is in a shroud. A brass indent from the same period in the nave of the church of St Mary at Southwick has a husband with his wife in a shroud, together with their children. More unusual are the depictions of both parents in shrouds, as at the east end of the nave of the church

One of a fine group of headstones at Titchmarsh, depicting Death pouring sand from an hourglass over the image of the deceased.

of St Mary at Burton Latimer, where part of a sixteenth-century brass showed what is believed to be Richard and Gresyll Boyvill, lord and lady of the manor, together with their nine sons. The remainder of the brass is still intact and shows their nine daughters.

One particularly striking image *is* intact and can be found on a hanging monument (1634) inside the chapel of St Peter at Steane. It depicts Temperance Brown sitting up in her coffin in a shroud. The rest of the composition has an angel with trumpet (symbolising victory over death), together with various allegorical figures.

JUDGEMENT DAY

The early Church employed a number of methods to ensure that the individual stayed true to the faith. For the majority, illiterate and unable to understand the Latin Mass, a series of striking visual images were designed to strike fear into the potential sinner, the most potent being the large Doom painting prominently situated above the chancel arch, in full view of the congregation. Full of demons, flames, punishments, groups of people being rounded up, and the gaping mouth of Hell – and also Christ, St Peter and the gates of Heaven – they were certainly an effective form of doctrine, along with the mystery/Corpus Christi plays. In this sense, 'doom' means 'judgement', a variation of its more common meaning, 'grim fate'. Doomsday is the final reckoning, when everyone is judged according to the way they have lived their lives (described in Revelation 20:12–15).

The concept of a Hell was only brought into official Christian doctrine at the Council of Constantinople in AD 547, and the Devil, previously a fallen 'angel' (his appearance and character defined at the Council of Toledo in AD 447), was later, from the twelfth century onwards, portrayed in animal and subsequently horned form when the established Church felt under threat from rival 'heretical' sects and non-existent covens of witches holding their own special forms of 'sabbat'. Hell was portrayed as a place full of fire and demons, where terrifying punishments were applied to the part of the body that had committed the sin(s) during one's lifetime. A vivid picture of the 'second death' is given in Revelation 21:8.

Wall paintings would have been produced using a lime wash, and, for the figures, red and yellow ochre (a mixture of clay and ferric oxide), charcoal for black, and the more expensive 'azur' or ultramarine from lapis lazuli for blue. They would periodically need repainting due to their transient nature, and being one of the first targets for elimination by the reformers under Edward VI and during the Civil War, they were whitewashed or scrubbed bare, hence no complete scenes survive today, leaving only fragmentary evidence of what once existed. Others have been discovered in more recent times, but as in the case of Easton on the Hill, where vestiges were visible in 1951, restoration or cleaning was deemed to be prohibitively expensive, and so nothing else was forthcoming. There are, however, fifteenth-century Doom painting fragments at Croughton and Irchester.

Better still are two more substantial versions in the county. That at Mears Ashby is divided into two halves, the damaged central/left-hand portion depicting Christ holding up his hands and showing his wounds, while above his head there is a partially legible banner, the cross and the keys of heaven; on the more preserved right-hand section is a group of monstrous figures pushing a group of sinners towards a winged monster with large eyes. The creature clutches one of them; a further cartload of sinners waits behind the group. Above, a horned demon prods a contorted figure headlong into the burning pit below.

At Great Harrowden, the faded but legible fifteenth-century Doom painting (in many respects one of the best preserved in England, in that vestiges of all the three main scenes are visible) shows Christ standing on a well-defined rainbow, displaying his wounds. Beside him stand the Virgin Mary and St John. An angel holds the cross, while another holds the lance that pierced Christ's side. Other angels sound the trumpet for the souls to rise up and await judgment, and they can be seen emerging from their graves on the left-hand side, some naked, others in their shrouds. The outlines of some of the figures here are distinct, almost engraved. St Peter is depicted above them, by the gates of Heaven, taking hold of one of those already judged. On the right-hand side of the painting, crowds of sinners are being lined up and cast into the gaping teeth-lined jaws of Hell. Sadly, much of the remainder of the painting has vanished.

Part of the medieval 'Doom' wall painting over the chancel arch in the church of All Saints at Mears Ashby.

Together, however, the paintings at Mears Ashby and Great Harrowden give an almost complete picture of how a complete Doom painting would have looked, although there is one important feature missing that can be found at two other churches in the county: St Michael weighing the souls in a balance, or scales, to determine which go to Heaven and which go to Hell.

On the wall of the south side of the nave at the wonderfully intact church of St Botolph at Slapton, part of the figure of St Michael has been lost (only his cloak/ lower half is now showing), but there is a clear image of the scales. In one of the pans sits a soul looking imploringly at the Virgin Mary, who is standing at the side. She was often present on the occasion, and being the Mother of God and the most influential of all holy figures, she was frequently seen as an intermediary, giving a last-minute reprieve for the truly penitent sinner if she touched the top of the scales with her hand or rosary, ensuring equal balance, as can be seen in the painting.

Another fairly good example (*c.* 1350) is on the north wall of the north aisle at the church of St Mary at Nassington. Here St Michael is clearly depicted, and most of the Virgin Mary can be seen on the right. Here she is touching the scale with her left hand, and with a gesture of the other hand seemingly giving the all-clear to St Michael for the soul in the pan beneath her. A smaller figure stands beneath the scales in a pleading posture. Beneath the scales where St Michael stands is a demon with clawed feet, also awaiting the outcome.

As at Slapton, the chancel arch was not the only place where scenes of the Last Judgment were depicted, one notable example being on the north wall of the nave of the church of St Peter at Raunds, where among a series of early fifteenth-century wall

Part of the medieval
wall painting of
St Michael weighing
souls in the church of
St Botolph at Slapton.

paintings is the image of Death piercing Pride (unusually in the form of a woman) with a lance, alongside dragons spewing out sins, and a sinner falling into the flaming jaws of Hell.

The instruments of the Passion are also depicted on the external walls of the unfinished Lyveden New Bield (1594–1605), commissioned by the recusant Sir Thomas Tresham. Among the images are the Cross, a ladder, hammer, tongs, lantern, scourge, sword, lances (one tipped with a sponge of gall) and anachronistic halberds (a combination of spear and battleaxe). Built as a symbol of passion, the original design was rejected by Tresham but used instead for a sister building to the Triangular Lodge at Rushton – the Hawkfield Lodge (1574, unfinished), which had disappeared by 1820.

RESURRECTION

A popular story acted out in the mystery plays but which does not appear in the Bible was the Harrowing of Hell by Christ. Although there are hints in the New Testament (in the epistles of Peter and the Ephesians), it is vividly described in the apocalyptic Gospel of Nicodemus, omitted with thirteen other Gnostic gospels from the official Biblical canon, but remaining very influential throughout the medieval period. It describes how Satan tells Hell to expect a very important 'guest', i.e. the newly crucified Christ. When the latter approaches, however, Hell begins to tremble with fear, and, on entering without encountering any obstacles, Christ leads the righteous – including Adam and the prophets – out of Hell. Satan is then seized and taken away to be dealt with in a punitive manner. There is a depiction of the scene among the superb set of early fourteenth-century wall paintings in the church of All Saints at Croughton. Others known to have existed elsewhere have unfortunately vanished.

A wall painting at Dodford shows a soul ascending into Heaven, while at the church of St Mary and All Saints at Holcot there are vestiges on another painting of the resurrection, although a rare example of the descent of the Holy Ghost has been allowed to fade away.

As the Reformation progressed, traditional *hope* of resurrection, with its bequests, was replaced by one of *certainty* of resurrection, and this is reflected in much of the newer imagery used in funerary art, although the earlier images of mortality still continued to play a part. One such example, depicting a range of resurrection images, can be found on the wall tablet of Magdalene Lant (*d.* 1694) in the church of Holy Trinity at Rothwell.

At Apethorpe there is rare stained glass from the seventeenth century. The third panel of four in the east window (1621) in the south chapel at the church of St Leonard depicts the ascension of Christ and bodies rising from the grave, with the words, 'He is the death of death, the life of the living and the quickener of the dead' and 'Thy dead men shall live.'

INFANT MORTALITY

For those of sufficient means, commemorating the loss of a child solely with an inscription was not a sufficient way of paying tribute or showing one's grief. The parents of Cilena l'Anson Bradley, who died at Long Buckby in 1726 aged twelve, commissioned an expensive bust of their daughter. Set within a square niche with a draped round head arch supported on pillars, it can be seen in the north choir vestry of the church. In the churchyard at Clipston, all other monuments are dwarfed by a tall, fluted pillar memorial on a large pedestal commemorating the death of Caelicia Floyer, the daughter of Charles Hogg and Louisa Fleming. She died at the age of fifteen months 'and twelve days' in November 1837.

Sometimes an image representing the child is portrayed. At Apethorpe, six-month-old John Fane (*d.* 1816, in Florence), the son of John Lord Burghersh, is depicted wearing a bonnet, with his eyes closed, and lying on a white marble mattress and couch. At Courteenhall, set within a niche, a porcelain effigy of a baby with its mouth open commemorates the short life of Iola Campbell, who died in 1852.

A child may also be depicted kneeling, as is the case with Richard Cave at Stanford, who died in Padua in 1606. At Crick, the child of Benjamin Button, a local stonemason, can be seen kneeling in prayer.

At the partially demolished church of Barnwell All Saints is an elaborate pyramidal obelisk decorated with wavy patterns in memory of the infant Henry Montagu, who drowned nearby in 1625, not yet three years old. There is also an image of a child surmounted by the word 'Jehovah' and open panels, one of which depicts the mantle

Incised images of children in swaddling clothes on the alabaster slab of the Tanfield tomb in the church of St Mary at Gayton.

that covered his hearse. An inscription briefly describes how the boy met his death while playing with the water in a 'scoopet'.

Other memorials, however, were of a different nature. A plain wall tablet in the north chapel of the church of St Peter at Lowick is poorly initialled and abbreviated in Latin. It is dedicated to William, the second son of John, 1st Earl of Peterborough. William died in infancy in 1625. In the chancel of the church of St Nicholas at Stanford, there is a small, unpretentious monument to Dorothy St John (*d.* 1630) with a black marble top, shields and garlands.

A rare type of tomb in Northamptonshire consisting of 'head, foot and body stone' lies in the churchyard north of the nave of the church at Oundle. The lettering, barely legible, dates from *c.* 1800 and is to an unknown child. Even earlier are two small medieval tombs of children in the churchyard at Wadenhoe, one of which was unearthed beside the north porch in 1993.

A graphic depiction of a dead mother and children on a headstone in the churchyard at Weedon Lois.

DEATH IN CHILDBIRTH

Of special interest is the number of chrisom babies in swaddling clothes – those that did not survive infancy. A brass in the chancel of the church of St Botolph at Barton Seagrave depicts twenty-eight-year-old Jane Floyde (*d.* 1616), the wife of the rector. She kneels at prayer, two surviving daughters behind her. Close by is a baby in a cot, with two others lying in their beds.

Another brass can be found set within a wall monument in the south aisle of the church of St Mary at Burton Latimer. It depicts Margaret Bacon, lady of the manor, who died four days after giving birth to her daughter in January 1626. The baby is also shown, lying beside her mother in swaddling clothes.

Depictions of where mother and baby have died are less common, but where they do occur they convey a sense of drama. On a headstone in the churchyard at Desborough (December 1796) is the well-preserved image of Ann Holmes holding her child, Harriet, by her side. Close to the chancel at Weedon Lois is the graphic view of a winged skull

A well-carved depiction of a dead mother and child on a slate headstone in the churchyard at Desborough.

gazing down from above at a dead mother, her child and a baby. At Towcester, there is a headstone (now face down) with a rare depiction of a naked mother with two children in her arms, together in death.

ALLEGORICAL FIGURES AND WEEPERS

There were a number of allegorical figures personifying the deceased's virtues and character in life, the most important of which was Charity, a female figure sometimes depicted with a heart and a flaming star. In addition there were seven Catholic virtues, which were always personified in female form (the vices were male). There were three theological virtues: Faith (Fides), depicted with a cross and a chalice; Hope (Spes), with anchor, crown or flag; and Love (Caritas), with a torch or lamb. In addition there were four cardinal virtues: Temperance, depicted with a skull and hourglass (as was the figure of Death), Justice, with sword and scales, Fortitude, and Prudence.

These virtues were often depicted on funerary monuments. A large number appear on the sumptuous marble tomb (1621) of Sir Anthony and Lady Grace Mildmay at Apethorpe, namely those of Faith, Hope, Piety, Justice, Wisdom and Charity (twice). The latter was certainly a characteristic trait of Lady Grace, who was renowned for her generosity in handing out money to the village children and providing food for the poor (she was even supposedly seen after her death, giving rise to one of the commonplace 'grey lady' sightings in folklore). From the mid-eighteenth century and the Neoclassic period, the most popular images in the county were those of Faith (as at Warkton, Great Brington, and Cottesbrooke) and Charity (Castle Ashby, and again at Great Brington and Warkton). Less common are images of Truth and Justice, which can be seen at Achurch (1719). In addition, there is a range of unnamed allegorical figures at Ashby St Ledger.

Among the earliest images, however, were 'weepers', or figures of mourning, which could be depicted in the form of family members, friends, saints, angels (all depicted on brasses and hanging monuments) and, particularly during the Baroque and Rococo era, winged cherubs and the 'putto'– a small naked boy (sometimes winged, like the cherub) derived from ancient representations of the Greek god of love Eros (i.e. the Roman god Cupid). He now acted in a subsidiary, attendant role. They can commonly be found all around the county, singularly or in groups, on monuments inside churches, such as those at Ashby St Ledger (1738), Steane (1697), Clipston (1706), Ecton (1763), Whiston (1792), Wicken (1726, 1747), Winwick (1707) and Rockingham (1724). On an early monument at Lamport (1638) they are shown holding wreaths. Part of a memorial dating from the fifteenth century and depicting two putti standing on skulls was found in the churchyard at Newnham and consequently taken into the church (its probable provenance).

The most common form of eighteenth-century weeper, however, especially on headstones, was the grieving female figure, in flowing classical gown, with her head inclined over an urn. There are excellent examples in the county's churchyards, such as Titchmarsh, Sudborough and Aldwincle All Saints.

NOTABLE MONUMENTS

Semi-reclining figures became popular in the seventeenth century and the fashion continued well into the following century. Most notable of all is that of Sir Arthur Throckmorton (d. 1626) and his wife Anne (d. 1629) in the north chapel of the church of St James the Great at Paulerspury. They are facing each other, their elbows almost touching, he with a smile on his face – a rare display of devotion in church statuary.

Portrait medallions with an image of the deceased were popular among more affluent families in the eighteenth century and usually formed part of a lavish sculptural composition or standing monument. There are typical examples at Warkton, Cottesbrooke, Grafton Underwood, Southwick, Great Brington, Stanford (two) and Clopton (two). Busts of the deceased were also fairly commonplace, as can be seen at Great Brington, Lamport and Ecton.

The composition and content of other, later, memorials are worth a brief mention. In the south aisle of the church at Stanford, a white marble memorial (1862) shows a young woman looking down sorrowfully at what is probably her mother, Sarah Braye. Beside her is a large cross propped against the wall, above are three winged cherubs.

The semi-reclining figures of Sir Arthur Throckmorton and his wife at Paulerspury (*c.* 1629).

At Easton Neston, George Fermor, 2nd Earl of Pomfret (*d.* 1785), was followed to the grave by his wife in 1787, but their memorial was only erected years later, in 1819. They are depicted bidding each other farewell, he wearing a loose robe in Greek style, she leaning towards him. At Farthinghoe, the monument of George Rush (*d.* 1806) depicts him as a reclining figure, looking up, wearing a nightcap, slippers and a loose robe, and holding a bible. In the north aisle of the church at Whittlebury, a marble wall tablet has Carolette Bradshaw in a long flowing diaphanous robe, her feet on an inscribed stone with the date of her death in Roman numerals (1820). She seems to glide upwards towards heaven.

A set of oak choir stalls in the choir of the church of St Nicholas at Twywell depicts Horace Waller, who was rector of the parish for twenty-one years, standing among slaves and a frieze of African animals. They were presented to the church in his memory in 1898. A friend of General Gordon and the explorer David Livingstone (whose journals he later edited), he was one of the first members of the Universities Mission to Central Africa.

Monuments can sometimes be found in isolation, usually at the site of an accidental death, just as flowers are placed by the site of roadside fatalities today. In a field overlooking the road between Pitsford and Brixworth is a tall, stepped pillar monument decorated with florets and topped by a gabled capital with heraldic shields. It was erected in memory of Charles, 3rd Lord Chesham, who met his death while riding with

Symbols of mortality: a woman pouring out her grief and a broken flowering stem.

the Pytchley Hunt in 1907. Yet another stepped pillar monument, with a Roman Ionic column, stands in the park of Stanford Hall in honour of Percy Pilcher, an aviation pioneer who died here in a flying machine accident at the age of thirty-two in 1899.

Memorials can also appear in a more secular form, two of which are at Kettering. One (*c.* 1907) is to Dr John Dryland, who was Medical Officer of Health and did much to improve the town's water supply. It is in the form of a drinking fountain (and formerly had adjacent horse troughs). Close by is a bronze bust of the renowned artist Alfred East (1849–1913), who gave the town the eponymous art gallery. By the side of the road in the hamlet of Achurch is a well-head decorated with Victorian tracery and angels, shaded by a hipped tiled roof with a wooden cross, below which is an inscription: 'In Memory of Thomas Atherton Powys, MDCCCLXXXII'. In the grounds of Althorp House is a planting stone in obelisk form, inscribed in memory of Margaret Spencer (1868–1906).

A BRIEF SUMMARY OF FUNERARY SYMBOLS

Untimely death was often depicted by a drooping, falling, or severed branch, bud or flower, or broken columns and pediments. Grief was a female figure bending over an urn, or depicted with a willow or drapery. The soul was often represented by a winged figure: birds (above all the dove, which also symbolised purity, love and the Holy

Spirit), the butterfly, or the winged angel head (the departing soul). An interesting early example can be found at Higham Ferrers where, among the images on the canopy of the altar tomb of Lawrence St Maur (1337), there is a soul held in a napkin by angels. At Dodford, a fourteenth-century painting depicts a soul being taken to heaven by angels and the hand of God.

Immortality was depicted in the form of an obelisk, pyramid, lamp or flaming torch; extinguished life by a downturned or extinguished torch. Resurrection was an angel's or cherub's head, a shell, a lion or an urn. Faith was a book. Reward and glory was a crown. Victory over death was represented by palms, laurels, cherubs with trumpets or a female figure holding a garland. Hope was commonly symbolised by rays of light or an anchor. Salvation is a cross or a heart. Truth and Knowledge are depicted with a mirror or a book. Memory is the book of life. Divine Love is a flaming heart. Sacrifice is a lamb (Agnus Dei).

OCCUPATIONAL

Not all memorials had images of death portrayed. Some were engraved with the tools and other items associated with a particular occupation. At Towcester a butcher, Sam Wood, had some of his tools engraved on a headstone (1820), which, like so many others in that churchyard, is now lying face-down. At Rothersthorpe, one side of the headstone of John Brett (*d.* 1753), a blacksmith, has a file and pincers, the other side a square and hammer. At Oundle, Robert Grooby (*d.* 1819) has three compasses, the arms of the Guild of Carpenters, engraved above his inscription.

One of the early nineteenth-century stonemasons at Oundle, Charles Braddock, has an eroding set square and compasses engraved on his headstone west of the church porch, as do William Sanderson at Yarwell (*d.* 1803) and John Coles at Islip (*d.* 1816). The images on the headstone of the latter have weathered particularly well. The arms of the Masons' Company are engraved on the tomb chests of John Wigson (*d.* 1713) and William Tew (*d.* 1717) at Eydon, as well as on the tomb chest of James Whiting (*d.* 1718) and headstone of Tubalcain Lumley (*d.* 1749), both at Harlestone.

There are also monuments without images but which mention the occupation of the deceased, as with that of Samuel Rippener (1778–1838) at Oundle. Others are more symbolic, depicting a broken pediment (i.e. an occupation brought to a halt by death), as on the 1623 wall memorial at Kingscliffe commemorating three generations of stonemasons, the Thorpe family (all of whom were named Thomas). At Weldon, however, the renowned stonemason families of Frisby and Grumbold have nothing more pretentious than plain chest tombs with their names and dates of death.

Worth visiting is the churchyard of Bisbrooke, just over the county boundary near Uppingham, where the uniquely decorative but deteriorating headstone of Nathaniel Clark, a carter who died in 1813, has a rural scene in which a cart is being drawn by four horses against a background of a mill, trees, gate and fencing.

The tradition of depicting associated tools of the trade has been continued in recent times at places like Southwick, where a hammer and saw have been depicted on the headstone of a village carpenter.

The headstone of John Coles, stonemason, at Islip, showing the tools of his trade.

WAR AND ACTIVE SERVICE

In churches all around the county there are monuments and wall tablets commemorating the premature deaths of those killed in various wars from the eighteenth to the twentieth centuries. After the First World War, a long-standing tradition of repatriation was abolished, most likely because of the unprecedented and horrific number of those slain. Communities, however, wanted to honour those who would never return, and between 1920 and 1921 many towns and villages built their own memorials, either in the church, churchyard or other public place, ranging from a simple roll of honour to a standard cross on a plinth or stepped base, a stone tablet set in an outside wall (as at Isham), an obelisk (as at Bozeat), and a tall Celtic cross with interlacing (as at Courteenhall and on the village green at Whittlebury). The most elaborate of all was an iron-gated shrine at Ecton, which was unique in being commissioned and erected in 1917 – *before* the end of the war. In most cases, the names of those who lost their lives in the Second World War were later added to existing memorials.

Like headstones, however, many war memorials have become neglected, or have become victims of the elements, vandalism and even partial theft. They have also had the disadvantage of not being listed and therefore have had little protection. Fortunately, some communities have acted and cleaned or even restored their memorials where it has been deemed necessary.

Some places had more than one monument, sometimes with ornate features, such as that in the High Street at Rothwell, where the top of the 19-foot-high war memorial has niches containing the figures of Peace, Victory, Christ at the Crucifixion and St George and the Dragon. At Higham Ferrers, near the old market cross, the memorial has the figure of an angel holding a laurel wreath carved in relief on one side, with the names of those killed in battle engraved in gold lettering below. The top of the pillar has the town coat of arms in colour.

In the Lady Chapel of the church at Desborough is a stained-glass window depicting St George with sword and shield looking at an inscription in memory of all those who fell in battle during the Second World War, in particular John Hawes, musician and poet, killed in action in 1943 at the age of twenty-five. The church also has an area of the south aisle, known as 'Hallelujah Corner', recording the names all those who fought in the First World War together with their regiments and honours. The names of all those killed during that war are recorded on the war memorial outside.

A wall monument in the tower of the church of St Andrew at Cotterstock commemorates John Simcoe, commander of HMS *Pembroke*, who died at the siege of Quebec in 1759. The battle also saw the death of General Wolfe and ultimately led to the formation of Canada. The ship is depicted in relief beneath the inscription, while on the wide obelisk surmounting the monument there are contemporary images of a keg of gunpowder, globe, telescope, blunderbuss, cannon balls, drum, sword and compass.

Luckier was Captain John Orme, who survived various battles and died at the age of seventy-eight in April 1764. His marble wall monument in the church at Polebrook depicts banners, cannon and a cavalry sword.

Edmund Verney, who was killed in action during the Anglo-Zulu War in South Africa in July 1879, is shown in the uniform of his regiment, the 17th Lancers, on a sumptuous monument in the church at Stanford. He is holding a wreath while gazing down at a Zulu shield. A bronze portrait medallion of him is affixed on a backing panel.

The church of the Holy Sepulchre in Northampton was formerly the garrison church of the Northamptonshire Regiment and therefore houses a great many funerary monuments in the chapel of St George, within which is the parochial war memorial with the names of those in the parish who died while on active service in gold lettering. It is surmounted by the figure of St George standing on a dragon. Commemorative stained-glass windows depict images of past heroes and martyrs: Henry V, St Alban, St Crispin, St Louis and St Martin. Elsewhere around the church are further stained-glass windows to individuals who lost their lives in battle during the First World War, while in the north aisle is a window dating from 1883, in memory of regimental comrades who were killed during the Anglo-Zulu and First Boer wars.

The Commonwealth Graves Commission (CGC) was established in 1917, and would go on to commemorate the 1,700,000 members of the Commonwealth forces who

A standard Commonwealth War
Graves Commission headstone of the
Northamptonshire Regiment.

died in both world wars. One of its tasks would be to honour each individual, where possible, by designing and producing a standardised vertical rounded-top headstone of white Portland stone engraved with the national emblem and regimental badge of the person at the top, and below this, his number and rank, name, unit/regiment, date of death, and age. Beneath these the appropriate religious symbol (cross, Star of David, etc.) was inscribed, and at the base a personal dedication chosen by relatives.

Men from all around the county enlisted in various regiments/units, including the Northamptonshire Regiment. One of the county's original units, the 58th Regiment of Foot (est. 1755), distinguished itself in two major periods of warfare: at the Great Siege of Gibraltar (1789–93), in which the Spanish tried to recover the rocky promontory that had been ceded to Britain at the Treaty of Utrecht following the War of the Spanish Succession (1701–14); and latterly during the Napoleonic Wars (1802–15), in which they fought during Wellington's campaign at Talavera against combined Spanish and French forces. The battle honours they received for their participation became part of their badge and insignia, which consequently appeared on the CGC headstones commemorating both world wars. The headstones depicted a castle and a key together with the words 'Gibraltar' and 'Talavera'. Although most of these are laid out in specially designated cemeteries in France and Belgium, isolated examples and those of other regiments in which county men served can be found in various churchyards around Northamptonshire.

From the summer of 1942 until 1945, the United States Army Air Force (USAAF) flew on countless missions from bases set up in the north of the county. After the war, four special memorials were set up along the road where four of these airfields had been sited, at Kingscliffe, Deenethorpe, Harrington and Grafton Underwood. The memorial at the latter village stands at the end of the former main runway on the road to Geddington. It was from here that the first and last missions by the USAAF were carried out by the 384th Bombardment Group between August 1942 and April 1945, in the course of which they lost a staggering 1,579 men. In the village church of St James, a stained-glass memorial window in the south aisle commemorates the memory of the men, depicting a B17 Flying Fortress returning home over the white cliffs of Dover after a long-range mission over Germany. There is a duplicate window in Utah.

One of the most unique memorials in the county can be found at Hellidon, in the form of a stained-glass 'portrait' window depicting the true-life images (taken from photographs) of four young men killed during the Great War.

7

WORKING IN STONE:
THE MASONS AND THEIR MATERIALS

Geologically, the county has been blessed with some of the best building stone in England, having both Lower and Upper Lincolnshire Limestone in the north of the county, Wellingborough and Helmdon limestone in the south and south-east, the less durable but extensive and attractive Northampton Sand ironstone, and, in the south-west of the county, marlstone, a calcareous form of ironstone. The limestone includes the rough, shelly Blisworth form and Barnack Rag (the latter used from the Roman era and into the medieval period), and the even-textured, less shelly Helmdon, Kingscliffe, Stanion and Weldon freestone (the latter used for the Eleanor Cross, many of the great buildings of the county and, further afield, Jesus College, the chapel of King's College and, supposedly, the original St Paul's Cathedral). The third kind is the fine, virtually shell-free Stamford and Ketton limestone, used mainly for ornamental features such as pillars, balustrades, pilasters, and some headstones. (A fissile form of limestone used for roofing was Collyweston 'slate', which was made in twenty-four sizes, each with its own unique name.) However, the most durable of any material for external use is Swithland slate, a metamorphic stone that hardly weathers, enabling inscriptions and depictions to be seen as clear as the day they were carved. It was popular and affordable in the Midlands from the late 1700s until its slow decline after the 1840s with the arrival of the railway, which enabled vast quantities of Welsh blue slate (as a roofing material) to be transported all over the country.

Occasionally one will see cast-iron grave markers covered in rust in the county's churchyards in place of stone. Smaller and cheaper, yet distinctive, they provided some form of monument to the less fortunate in the community. Examples can be found at Rushton, Desborough and Laxton. Wood would have been used in many places in the early days of grave markers in the seventeenth century, but these have long since perished, and are therefore unknown in Northamptonshire (although they can still be seen in the southern counties in the form of graveboards). Portland stone, a much-prized form of limestone from the south coast, was the prescribed fabric for the CGC headstones erected for those who lost their lives in the two world wars.

Other types of stone from outside the county have been used for internal funerary monuments. Purbeck 'marble', a form of limestone that can be given a polished look like real marble, was popular among the more affluent until it was overtaken by alabaster, a form of gypsum, from the Derbyshire area. This soft stone was used for internal monuments from the fifteenth century; it is easy to carve and has a distinctive colouring, although the clothing of effigies was often painted in bright colours. It was also a target over the centuries for those wishing to while away a little time practising their graffiti 'skills', as can be seen on a great number of altar tombs.

Clunch, a form of hard chalk, has been used for some monuments as it is ideal for carving finer or more intricate features. Good examples are in the Spencer chapel at Great Brington and at Fotheringhay, where, latterly it has been used with limestone on the York family's wall monuments.

Another fabric used in funerary monuments, although usually for smaller features like urns or busts, was terracotta, hard-baked clay that has been used for this purpose since ancient times. It can be seen in a variety of colours, which are determined by the chemical composition of the clay or the type of firing process involved. There are good examples inside the church at Ecton and in the churchyard at Quinton.

An artificial stone known as Coade Stone – a form of cast terracotta containing ground glass and quartz – was developed in London, and was used from 1769 until 1840. Being mixed as a paste and shaped in moulds, it could be mass-produced in identical forms, thereby proving very popular, both inside and out (where it was virtually frost-free). One particular sculptor renowned for its use was John Bacon (senior), who worked for the company that had invented and manufactured the stone. There are a few examples in county churches, such as the wall monument to Mary Poulton (*d.* 1779) in the chancel of St Giles in Desborough, and that of Sir William Langham (*d.* 1815) in the nave of the church of All Saints at Cottesbrooke.

It was marble, however, that became the most desirable stone for funerary sculpture, particularly during the eighteenth century, initially with the Rococo and (more importantly) the later Neoclassical styles. The best stone was imported from Greece and Italy (particularly Carrera), although there were also fine quarries in Devon and Derbyshire. A form of limestone that has had its structure recrystallised by natural heat and pressure, transforming it into a hard, durable fabric, marble can be found in pure white form or in a variety of colours such as grey, black, pink and beige, and a range of patterns. Early examples of its use can be found on the expensive, sumptuously carved monuments at Church Stowe (1620, made during the lifetime of its commissioner, Lady Carey), the Mildmay monument at Apethorpe (1621), and one of the Spencer family monuments at Great Brington (1638).

THE FUNERARY MASONS OF NORTHAMPTONSHIRE

The quality of a mason's work would be determined by a variety of factors: his knowledge, his skills, the type of stone being used, the amount of time spent in production, and perhaps more importantly, how much money was received for each commission – the more elaborate the images or calligraphy, the higher the cost. Funerary masons had pattern books from which a customer could choose a motif or verse, just like today's product catalogues, and they normally advertised their work by including their trademark at the base of a headstone – usually their name engraved with simple lettering.

Northamptonshire was home to dynasties of renowned stonemasons such as the Ireson family, first recorded in 1658, who worked in much of the northern part of the county in places such as Bulwick, Kettering, Nassington, Oundle, Thrapston, Yarwell and Apethorpe (where William Ireson carved his initials and the date 1776 on the east face of the south porch). The family flourished well into the twentieth century. In the south of the county at Helmdon was the Campium family, one member of which, William, is depicted working on a stone with his pick on a fourteenth-century stained-glass window in the village church. The Lumley family of masons was active in the Harlestone area from the sixteenth century for almost 250 years. At Weldon in the sixteenth and seventeenth centuries were the Frisby and Grumbold families, who intermarried and whose homes, which they elaborately crafted, designed and decorated, can still be seen, constructed of fine ashlar limestone excavated from their nearby quarries. They are, namely, 'Haunt Hill House' (built between 1636 and 1643) and what is now 25 High Street (dating from 1654). Equally fine tombs of family members stand in the village churchyard. Over at Kingscliffe, three generations of the Thorpe family, all named Thomas, were active during the sixteenth and seventeenth centuries, counting among their work Kirby Hall, Rothwell Market House and Dingley Hall (where there is a wall tablet in the village church to the three men, dated 1623). The Streather family at Corby produced a dynasty of masons from the mid-1700s until the early years of the twentieth century.

However, it is funerary masons we are concerned with here. Considered a specialist branch since the medieval era, when they carved coffin lids and altar tombs, they developed and refined their art and skills when new styles were introduced and according to changes of fashion. Among the earliest specialists were those based at the Barnack quarries from the eleventh century, who produced a distinctive style of early medieval coffin lids.

Top of the list of renowned carvers in the county were the Cox family of Northampton and Daventry, who flourished between the early 1700s and the 1850s. The dynasty was established by Samuel Cox (1690–1749), who came from a family of carpenters living at Hanslope in Buckinghamshire, just over the county border, where elaborate tombs of some members were carved with tools of their trade. He came to live at Derngate in Northampton and soon gained a reputation in the town and vicinity for the skill and quality of his work, especially with interior cartouches, tablets, 'broken pediments' and oval monuments. Two of his sons, William (1717–93) and Henry (1725–1810), enhanced their father's reputation, their speciality being the marble 'pyramid' monument, which he had produced in 1741 for the church of All Saints in the town. Their work can also be seen in places such as Braybrooke, Guilsborough, Piddington and Potterspury. Their own sons, Samuel (d. 1772) and William (d. 1784), followed their example but lived and worked in the Daventry area, some of their products being at Cold Higham and Welton. They were also commissioned for work in Kingsthorpe and Northampton. Samuel's son, also named Samuel (1767–1857), was the last of the dynasty, continuing his father's work around Daventry.

Another Northampton-based carver was John Hunt, who proudly asserted that he had served his apprenticeship under Grinling Gibbons (1648–1721), a skilled sculptor and woodcarver who had worked at St Paul's Cathedral, and who had been chief engraver to the artist Geoffrey Kneller. An advertisement for his occupation appeared in July 1751 in the *Northampton Mercury*, describing himself as 'statuary and carver in wood and stone'. Examples of his work can be seen in various churches in Northampton, and in the villages of Barton Seagrave (a 1724 wall tablet to John Bridges, the county historian, who had been born in the village), Finedon, Long Buckby, Overstone, Paulerspury, and in the Victoria and Albert Museum (a wall tablet from the demolished church at Faxton).

County stonemasons were certainly aware of the respective skills of their fellow craftsmen and this could be a determining factor in commissioning funerary monuments for their own decease. Henry Cox was so well esteemed that a Paulerspury stonemason, Joshua Lepper, stipulated in his will (1762) that a pair of headstones were to be carved and erected at a cost of three guineas by Cox, if he was still alive at the time, or failing that, by 'some other good carver'.

The list below shows other notable county funerary masons. Many were based at the villages and towns below but have examples of their work in other churchyards. Richard Dams, for example, was active at Kettering, Wilbarston and Market Harborough.

- Barnwell St Andrew: Daniel Stevens (1724–78), Daniel Stevens (1814–80)
- Clipston: Robert Weddington (1717–91), William Bonser (*c.* 1789–1857), Charles Cooke (*c.* 1750–1800)
- Cottingham: William Simpson (1804–87), John Simpson (1827–1900)
- Easton on the Hill: William Perkins (nineteenth century).
- Islip and Thrapston: John Coles (1736–1816), James Coles (1791–1834)
- Kettering: Richard Dams (*c.* 1797–1851); Joseph and William Bayes (*fl.* 1830)
- Maidwell: William Bland (1658–1703)
- Middleton Cheney: Thomas Williams (*fl.* 1741–69)
- Oundle: Samuel Rippener (*c.* 1800–38), Samuel (junior) and John Rippener (*fl.* 1841–70), Thomas Swann (*fl.* 1841–77), Charles Braddock (*c.* 1795–1830)
- Rothwell: George Dawkins (1731–91) and his son William (1773–1852), Charles, George and William Cook (*fl.* 1760s–1859), Edward, Samuel, Thomas and George Barlow (*fl. c.* 1760–*c.* 1880), John and Stephen Essex (*fl.* 1750–1850)
- Rushden: Thomas Margetts (*fl.* 1825–53)
- Stoke Albany: William Chapman (*fl.* 1840s)
- Scaldwell: William Kiteley (*c.* 1791–1846)
- Thrapston: Charles Horn (*fl.* 1808–35), James Coles (*fl.* 1800–40, also active at Wellingborough), Richard and Jonathan Bland (*fl.* mid-1700s–*c.* 1800), Thomas Barlow (*c.* 1810–70).
- Towcester: John Middleton (1749–1805), John Jeffs (1791–1867), Charles Cakebread (*fl.* 1872–89), William Thomason (1798–1838).
- Ufford: Robert Smyth (1763–1837)

The signature of Charles Cooke on the base of a headstone at Desborough.

- Weldon: John and William Goodliff (*fl.* 1830s)
- Yarwell: William Sanderson (1763–1803)

Funerary masons living on the periphery of Northamptonshire were also active in the county at various times during their working lives. Among them were: William and James Hill of Great Easton, who worked in the area between 1727 and 1763; the Clarke family of Liddington (John, Joseph, Robert and Robert Jr), who operated in the years between 1766 and 1871; Henry Smith of Elton, 1764–1836; Robert Goodwin of Stamford, 1793–1842; William Gilbert, 1783–1863 and his son Thomas, 1811–74; and Thomas Eldridge of Lubbenham, between 1820 and 1835. Additionally, John Wing of Leicester was working regularly at Maidwell between 1782 and 1792. Also active in the county during the eighteenth century were William Bonser of Burton Overy, members of the Leicestershire-based Ferriman family, *c.* 1715–80, and Henry Clay of Leicester.

One remarkable man, Samuel Turner, was born in Northamptonshire at Harrington but spent most of his life in Market Harborough as a shepherd, engraver and surveyor. He produced outstanding carvings in the area. His own 1784 headstone in the now-redundant churchyard of St Mary in Arden gives some idea of the quality of his work, being engraved with a sundial, the words 'Tempus Fugit', surveyor's instruments and biographical details. Another fine example of his work, from 1791, can be seen at Desborough.

8

TOLLING THE BELLS

Bells were always a vital form of communication. They were used not just for summoning the population to church for Mass and other services, but for announcing or celebrating nationally important events such as a military victory and royal or society weddings, as well as for local daily necessities such as curfew, or seasonal customs such as gleaning. Here, of course, we are concerned with burials. One of the bells at the church of All Saints at Norton is fittingly engraved: 'To the Church the Liveing I Do Call, The Dead to the Grave I Summon All.'

Whenever there was a death, church bells had a kind of media role. Depending on who you were and where you were living at the time, the whole village or town was informed of the fact that someone had died (after news had been received by a church official, usually a churchwarden) and the death knell would be rung. When someone was to be buried, the normal toll for most churches in the county would be three times for a man, twice for a woman and once for a child, but there were some variations.

At Brackley, Great Oakley and Benefield, the norm was thrice three times for a man, thrice two times for a woman, and three single tolls for a child. Duddington was unique; a bell was tolled for each of the years a child had lived before its death, while at Helmdon and Sudborough bells would be tolled for a whole hour for an adult and half an hour for a child. Towcester would toll five times for a man and four for a woman, with bells rung for children under twelve, while in the twin parishes at Cranford, bells were rung five times for a man, four for a woman, three for a boy and two for a girl. At Slipton, no distinction was made between man or woman.

At Oundle and in some villages such as Lowick and Twywell, an additional bell could be tolled for each year of the deceased's life, if so requested by relatives. At Kingscliffe, an additional 'winding bell' was rung when the body was put in a shroud. At Benefield, the bells were tolled both before and after the funeral, while at villages such as Bulwick and Cottingham, the bells were tolled as the funeral procession approached the church. It was usual at East Farndon after the standard death knell to toll for the pall bearers, relatives and friends, and again when the funeral procession left the house where the body lay.

Special treatment was given at Hellidon for the deceased member of any family that had long been established in the village – a short peal was given after the service. At Raunds, a small bell would be rung after the normal tolls, according to age and sex.

Aldwincle St Peter was particularly unique, in that bells would never be rung before sunrise or after sunset, regardless of any death occurring within that period.

In the towns there was a more elaborate system. At Daventry the 'third bell' was tolled thirty-two times for a man, thirty times for a woman, twenty-six times for a young man, twenty-four for a young woman, eighteen for a boy and sixteen for a girl, and then the tenor bell was tolled before and after a funeral. Towcester would toll five times for a man, and four for a woman; the third bell would be tolled for a child under twelve years old (at Kettering, the seventh bell would be used). At Wellingborough (and also at Bulwick and Cottingham) the tenor bell would be rung for fifteen minutes as the funeral procession made its way to the church. At Finedon, there were nine tolls for a man and seven for a woman, on each of its six bells.

All of these customary practices had begun to die out by the end of the Victorian era. Twywell, where funeral chimes ceased in 1862, is a typical example.

APPENDIX 1

BRASSES

The following is a list of those churches with one *illustrated* brass (floor, wall or on altar tomb) and their approximate dates. It does not include inscription-only brasses:

Aldwincle All Saints: 1463
Ashton (near Roade): 1584
Aston le Walls: 1609
Barnwell All Saints: 1610
Barton Seagrave: 1616
Blakesley: 1416
Blatherwycke: 1548
Blisworth: 1504
Canons Ashby: 1584
Castle Ashby: 1401
Chacombe: 1569
Church Brampton: 1585
Collyweston: 1508
Cotterstock: 1420
Dingley: 1577
Earls Barton: 1512
East Farndon: 1622
Easton Neston: 1552
Great Addington: 1519
Great Harrowden: 1424
Grendon: 1480
Harrington: 1545
Hemington: 1517

Horton: 1491
Irchester: 1506
Islip: 1911
Kelmarsh: 1534
Kettering: 1630
Lowick: 1467
Marholm: 1534
Naseby: 1446
Nether Heyford: 1487
Newbottle: 1555
Newnham: *c.* 1467
Northampton Holy Sepulchre: 1640
Norton: 1501
Orlingbury: 1502
Spratton: 1464
Staverton: 1580
Sudborough: 1415
Sulgrave: 1584
Tansor: 1440
Upper Boddington: 1627
Welford: 1585
Woodford (near Thrapston): 1580
Woodford Halse: 1425

The following churches have more than one illustrated brass, again with approximate dates:

Ashby St Ledger: 1416, 1494, 1505, 1506, 1510
Brampton Ash: 1420, 1468

Burton Latimer: 1500, 1600
Charwelton: 1490, 1490, 1541
Chipping Warden: 1468, 1584

Cranford St Andrew: *c.* 1418, *c.* 1602
Cransley: 1515, 1589
Deene: 1584, 1586, 1606 (two from Newton)
Dodford: 1414, 1422, 1637
Fawsley: 1516, *c.* 1557
Flore: 1450, 1510, 1537
Geddington : 1400, 1604, 1480
Greens Norton: 1462, 1490
Higham Ferrers: 1337, 1400, 1425, 1435, 1498, 1500, 1501, 1504, 1540

Newton Bromswold: 1426, 1487
Raunds: 1470, *c.* 1500, 1632
Rothwell: 1361, 1514, 1591
Tansor: 1440, 1913
Wappenham: 1460, 1481, 1499, *c.* 1500, *c.* 1500
Warkworth: 1412, 1420, 1420, 1430, 1454

APPENDIX 2

HATCHMENTS

The following list shows those hatchments that are still visible today. Many have since disappeared, however (and continue to do so):

Aldwincle All Saints: 1
Ashby St Ledger: 8
Benefield: 1
Blatherwycke: 3
Brockhall: 4
Canons Ashby: 11
Catesby: 2
Courteenhall: 4
Deene: 1
East Carlton: 6
Easton Maudit: 4
Easton Neston: 5
Easton on the Hill: 1
Everdon: 1
Fawsley: 3
Great Brington: 8
Great Oakley: 5
Grendon: 3
Hardingstone: 3
Harleston: 2
Harringworth: 1
Haselbech: 1
Horton: 1

Lamport: 1
Litchborough: 3
Lowick: 2
Marston Trussell: 1
Middleton Cheney: 4
Norton: 6
Polebrook: 1
Preston Deanery: 2
Ravensthorp: 2
Rothwell: 5
Stamford St Martin: 4
Stanford: 17
Stoke Bruerne: 1
Thenford: 1
Twywell: 1
Ufford: 2
Upton: 4
Wadenhoe: 1
Weedon Lois: 3
West Haddon: 1
Whiston: 3
Wollaston: 1
Yardley Hastings: 1

Hatchments recorded elsewhere:

Boughton House: 1
Harrowden Hall: 1
Lower Heyford House: 1

Thorpe Malsor Hall: 1
Welton Place: 3

APPENDIX 3

RECUMBENT STONE EFFIGIES

There are 121 medieval stone effigies surviving in the county, some of the most significant of which are listed here, according to the type of material used in construction. These were completed up to seven years after death, sometimes even later, when a spouse was added.

Purbeck marble:
c. 1268: Sir David de Esseby (Castle Ashby)
c. 1287: Sir Gerard de L'Isle (Church Stowe)
c. 1296: Sir William de Goldingham (Rushton)
1350: Sir John de Pateshull (Cold Higham)

Limestone:
1250: Robert de Vere (Sudborough)
c. 1280: Sir Nicholas de Cogenhoe
c. 1310: Mabila de Murdak (Gayton)
c. 1340: The wife of Sir Richard de Wade (Eydon)
c. 1345: Scholastica de Gayton (Gayton)
c. 1346: Sir William de Henton and wife (Hinton in the Hedges)
c. 1348: John de Ardele (Aston le Walls)
1376: Wentiliana de Keynes (Dodford)

Barnack ragstone:
1296: Sir John de Verdon (Brixworth)
c. 1300: Female effigy, believed to be a member of the de Bernack family (Barnack)

Red sandstone:
c. 1300: Member of the de Ros family (Braunston)
1330: Maud Holland (Woodford Halse)
1365: Sir John de Herteshall (Ashton near Roade)

Clunch:
fl. 1346: Sir John de Lyons (Warkworth)

c. 1410: Sir John de Whittelbury (Marholm)
15th/16th centuries: Spencer family chapel, eight effigies (Great Brington)

Alabaster:
1371: Sir John Swinford (Spratton)
c. 1375: Unknown figure of a knight (Orlingbury)
c. 1380: John and Joan Pywell (Irthlingborough)
1419: Sir Ralph and Katherine Green (Lowick)
1442: Sir Richard Dalton (Apethorpe)
1444: Sir John Cressy (Dodford)
1457: Sir Thomas and Philippa Green (Greens Norton)
c. 1490: Effigy of an unknown female (Irthlingborough)
1534: Sir Richard and Jane Knightley (Fawsley)
c. 1564: Sir Thomas, Katherine and Mary Andrewes (Charwelton)

APPENDIX 4

PARISH REGISTERS

The keeping of parish registers theoretically began in 1538. During the Dissolution of the Monasteries between 1536 and 1541, Henry VIII's chief minister, Thomas Cromwell, ordered all church incumbents to keep an annual record of births, marriages and deaths in each community. However, in most cases, these were initially recorded on loose sheets of paper, which were kept and stored in a haphazard and negligent manner, leading to loss or destruction. In later times some were reputedly cut into pieces and used as jam pot covers by the wives of various incumbents, while others were used to start household fires. In Northamptonshire, records survive in only eleven parishes from that year, these being Barby, Blakesley, Braunston, Courteenhall, Eydon, Hannington, Harpole, Kislingbury, Maxey, Newbottle, and Spratton. Complete records, therefore, are relatively uncommon. However, this had not gone unnoticed by the authorities, and sixty years later in 1598, they ordered the records to be kept in parchment books, which were to be retained in a proper place of storage, ideally the parish chest.

That being said, many villages in the county only have records beginning in the seventeenth and eighteenth centuries, and two, Thenford and Warkworth, in 1812 and 1814 respectively. The full list is shown below, with the earliest known date for each parish.

All this can be frustrating, but nevertheless what survives can be very rewarding. The registers are an ideal way of tracing missing detail on eroded or partly legible inscriptions on headstones. The entries are usually in clear English and, depending on the minister, sometimes include an additional comment about the person, such as cause of death, as seen in the following examples:

- 'Richard Tomason falling out of a tree as he was gathering ivie vpon the Lordes day, tooke his death wound and was buried the xxij month of December.' (Blakesley, 1601)
- 'Ann Hamblin, wife to Addam, he knockt her on the hed on the 8 of December & shee was buried on ye 11 of December.' (Nassington, 1625)
- 'Buried. Robert the sonne of ffrancis Whitewell. The nose eaton of wth a ferret & killed the child.' (Nassington, 19 September 1645)
- 'Buried. William Blofield, found in Titchmarsh meadow perished by severe frost.' (Islip, 10 January 1763)
- 'George Ease Taylor of Sudboro' being indisposed, thought bathing might be of service, he accordingly went to the river alone, stripped and leap'd into a pit above the mill and was drowned.' (Islip, 26 March 1783)

- 'It is remarkable that this man has not been seen in a place of worship for thirty years before he dyd.' (William Sturgis, sixty-nine, Clipston, 15 December 1792)
- 'She was blind for the last 4 years of her life, yet she got her livelihood by spinning flax. Her blindness was accidental ... in attempting to raise a large piece of meat out of a pot, it slipped and the fork recoiled with such violence to the eye that it soon lost its sight, and the anguish affected the other eye, so that she became totally blind.' (Mary York, sixty-four, Clipston, 1794)

The registers also include occasional quirky entries, such as that for a baptism at Kingsthorpe in 1600, where the vicar, either with a touch of irony, humour or guesswork wrote: 'Alice Noname, daughter of Nicholas Nobody, was baptised the 26th March.'

THE PARISH REGISTERS OF NORTHAMPTONSHIRE

Abington 1637, Abthorpe 1583, Achurch 1591, Adstone 1678, Alderton 1597, Aldwincle 1653, Apethorpe 1676, Arthingworth 1650, Ashby St Ledgers 1554, Ashley 1588, Ashton (near Roade) 1682, Aston le Walls 1538, Aynho 1562, Badby 1559, Barby 1538, Barnwell All Saints 1695, Barnwell St Andrew 1558, Barton Seagrave 1609, Benefield 1570, Blakesley 1538, Blatherwycke 1621, Blisworth 1548, Boddington 1558, Boughton 1549, Bozeat 1729, Brackley St Peter 1560, Bradden 1754, Brafield 1653, Brampton Ash 1580, Braunston 1538, Braybrooke 1653, Brigstock 1641, Brixworth 1546, Brockhall 1561, Broughton 1560, Bugbrooke 1556, Bulwick 1568, Burton Latimer 1538, Byfield 1636, Canons Ashby 1696, Castle Ashby 1564, Catesby 1705, Chalcombe 1566, Charwelton 1697, Chelveston 1572, Church Brampton 1561, Chipping Warden 1579, Clay Coton 1541, Clipston 1667, Clopton 1558, Cogenhoe 1560, Cold Ashby 1560, Cold Higham 1683, Collingtree 1802, Collyweston 1541, Corby 1684, Cosgrove 1691, Cotterstock 1783, Cottesbrooke 1630, Cottingham 1577, Courteenhall 1538, Cranford At Andrew 1695, Cranford St John 1627, Cransley 1561, Crick 1559, Croughton 1663, Culworth 1563, Dallington 1577, Daventry 1560, Deene 1588, Denford 1596, Denton 1540, Desborough 1571, Dingley 1583, Dodford 1581, Draughton 1559, Duddington 1733, Duston 1692, Earls Barton 1558, East Carlton 1625, East Farndon 1562, Easton Maudit 1539, Easton Neston 1559, Easton on the Hill 1579, Ecton 1559, Edgcote 1717, Everdon 1558, Evenley 1694, Eydon 1538, Farthinghoe 1560, Farthingstone 1538, Fawsley 1585, Faxton 1568, Finedon 1539, Flore 1652, Fotheringhay 1557, Furtho 1696, Gayton 1558, Geddington 1700, Glapthorn 1583, Gretton 1556, Grafton Regis 1584, Grafton Underwood 1678, Greatworth 1754, Greens Norton 1565, Great Addington 1692, Great Billing 1662, Great Brington 1558, Great Creaton 1688, Great Doddington 1560, Great Harrowden 1672, Great Houghton 1558, Great Oakley 1562, Great Oxendon 1565, Grendon 1559, Guilsborough 1560, Hannington 1538, Hardingstone 1562, Hardwick 1559, Hargrave 1572, Harlestone 1570, Harpole 1538, Harrington 1673, Harringworth 1695, Hartwell 1682, Haselbech 1653, Hellidon 1582, Helmdon 1582, Hemington 1574, Higham Ferrers 1579, Hinton in the Hedges 1558, Holcot 1559, Holdenby 1754, Horton 1603, Irchester 1622, Irthlingborough 1562, Isham 1701, Islip 1695, Kelmarsh 1599, Kettering 1637, Kilsby 1758, Kings Cliffe 1690, Kings Sutton 1570, Kingsthorpe 1540, Kislingbury 1538, Lamport 1587, Laxton 1689, Lilbourne 1573, Lilford 1560, Litchborough 1732, Little Addington 1588, Little Billing 1632, Little Bowden 1653, Little Harrowden 1653, Little Houghton 1540,

Little Oakley 1679, Loddington 1622, Long Buckby 1588, Lowick 1542, Luddington in the Brook 1672, Lutton 1653, Maidford 1711, Maidwell 1708, Marston St Lawrence 1559, Marston Trussell 1561, Mears Ashby 1670, Middleton Cheney 1558, Milton 1558, Moreton Pinkney 1641, Moulton 1565, Naseby 1563, Nassington 1560, Nether Heyford 1558, Newbottle 1538, Newnham 1568, Newton (in the Willows) 1660, Newton Bromswold 1560, Northampton All Saints 1560, Northampton Holy Sepulchre 1566, Northampton St Giles 1559, Northampton St Peter 1578, Norton 1678, Old 1559, Orlingbury 1564, Oundle 1625, Overstone 1673, Passenham 1695, Pattishall 1556, Paulerspury 1557, Piddington 1573, Pilton 1569, Pitsford 1560, Plunpton 1682, Polebrook 1653, Potterspury 1674, Preston Capes 1613, Preston Deanery 1676, Pytchley 1695, Quinton 1648, Radstone 1565, Raunds 1581, Ravensthorpe 1539, Ringstead 1570, Roade 1587, Rockingham 1562, Rothersthorpe 1563, Rothwell 1614, Rushden 1559, Rushton 1559, Scaldwell 1560, Shutlanger 1560, Sibberton 1680, Silverstone 1831, Slapton 1573, Slipton 1571, Southwick 1732, Spratton 1538, Stamford St Martin 1572, Stanford 1701, Stanion 1653, Stanwick 1558, Staverton 1564, Steane 1697, Stoke Albany 1575, Stoke Bruerne 1560, Stoke Doyle 1560, Stowe Nine Churches 1560, Strixton 1730, Sudborough 1660, Sulgrave 1668, Sutton Bassett 1576, Syresham 1668, Sywell 1571, Tansor 1639, Thenford 1812, Thornby 1649, Thorpe Malsor 1538, Thorpe Mandeville 1559, Thurning 1560, Thrapston 1560, Tiffield 1559, Towcester 1561, Twywell 1586, Upton 1594, Wadenhoe 1559, Wakerley 1540, Walgrave 1571, Wappenham 1678, Warkton 1559, Warkworth 1814, Warmington 1558, Watford 1565, Weedon Bec 1587, Weedon Lois 1559, Weekley 1550, Weldon 1594, Welford 1562, Wellingborough 1576, Welton 1578, West Haddon 1653, Weston by Welland 1576, Weston Favell 1540, Whilton 1570, Whiston 1700, Whitfield 1581, Whittlebury 1653, Wicken 1559, Wilbarston 1746, Wilby 1562, Winwick 1567, Wollaston 1663, Woodford 1680, Woodford Halse 1602, Woodnewton 1558, Wootton 1701, Yardley Hastings 1550, Yelvertoft 1573.

And in the Soke of Peterborough:

Bainton 1713, Barnack 1696, Castor 1538, Etton 1587, Eye 1543, Glinton 1567, Helpston 1685, Marholm 1566, Maxey 1538, Northborough 1671, Paston 1644, Peakirk 1560, Peterborough Cathedral 1615, Peterborough St John the Baptist 1558, Sutton 1758, Thornhaugh 1562, Ufford 1570, Upton 1770, Wansford 1898, Wittering 1648.

A PASTOR'S JOURNAL

The second pastor of Rothwell Independent Church was one of the most pious and perhaps over-zealous Puritan ministers of the seventeenth century. One particular entry in his journal for 14 March 1658 may seem to modern eyes somewhat unfeeling and unchristian. He wrote dismissively about the death of a child of one of the townspeople, justifying the death 'by God's stroke' and castigating its father: 'a little before he had scornfully objected to me that I had no children, nor never would, when I reproved him for no better educating his'. He described the father as 'a most desperate loose sinner and opposer of my ministry who had not been humbled by the loss of a child … [after overdrinking] he ran mad at me, stripped naked, with a drawn knife in his hand as to have done me hurt on purpose, so yt was the devil in him …' The father inflicted no injury and later regretted his hot-tempered behaviour.

FIELD NAMES

Sometimes names can be misleading. A classic example, at one time misinterpreted, was 'Dedequenemor', recorded in a thirteenth-century document discovered in 1907 concerning the Whittlebury area. It was speculated that it may have referred to Boudicca or an unknown queen. However, the word 'cwene' in Old English ('quene' in Middle English) meant 'lady' or 'wife'. Today, the word is still used in Scandinavia for 'woman' ('kvinna' in Swedish, 'kvinde' in Danish). Thus the reference is to (waste) land belonging to an unspecified deceased woman.

The strange-looking 'Dead Shells' at Welton is another example of an archaic word that has been transmuted, by dialect and time, into something seemingly unrelated. It is not a reference to fossils or molluscs, but to land belonging to a particular dead man. The name originated with an old Germanic word, 'carl' ('man'), which in the medieval period became 'churl', a peasant, hence it was applied to land belonging to the local man to whom it belonged. There are more straightforward examples elsewhere in the county referring to land belonging to, or containing the body of, a certain person. These include 'Deadman's Grave' (grove) at Warmington and Kislingbury. The latter, also known as Knitter's Grave, was believed to be the burial place of a local man, Richard Taylor, who took his life there by swallowing poison. At Hollowell there was 'Deadman', while at Brixworth in the fourteenth century there was 'Dedemansbyryellys' – i.e. a dead man's burial place. In Northampton, there is a reference in 1247 to 'Dedemanes Twichene' (the Old English 'twicene' means 'crossways'), which is likely to have been a crossroads burial site for criminals and suicides.

Similarly, 'Cut Throat Field' (and Cut Throat Lane), a name once found in the county, such as at Great Doddington, has nothing to do with the site of a murder, but is simply a garbled version, once again via dialect, of 'cut through field' hence a shortcut. At Brigstock, there was formerly 'Blood and Guts Row', a nickname for a place where poachers would bury evidence or remains of their forages.

Other sites are more straightforward, such as 'Gib Hill' at Hollowell, named after the execution (and subsequent display on a gibbet) of a murderer there in 1764. There is also 'Gallows Hill' at Rushden, 'Gallows Bank' at Kilsby and 'Gallows Field' at Stuchbury. At Gretton, there is a 'Gallows Hill', which may also have been named for this purpose. 'Hangman's Barn' at Spratton, however, is a reference to a place of ownership or the perquisite of a local executioner.

An alternative name for 'Pudding Bag' at Marston Trussell was 'Cavaliers' Grave', for it was here that several Royalist troops fleeing the battlefield at Naseby in 1649 were hemmed in and cut down by pursuing Parliamentarian troops, and buried in a mass grave in the adjoining churchyard of St Nicholas. A ford across the River Welland, close to the massacre, is still known as 'Slaughterford'.

The strangely named 'Tom Tom Corner' in Wadenhoe parish is said to be the place where two local boys, both named Tom, were playing with a group of other village lads during a summer thunderstorm when they were struck by lightning and instantly killed.

Haunt Hill at Weldon is supposedly the place where a nun was murdered in the medieval period, and whose apparition, in the form of a white figure floating around the vicinity, was frequently sighted. Her bloodstains were said to have indelibly marked the flagstones of the floor of the building in which she met her end. Unfortunately it could not have been the present Haunt Hill House – it was built years later, between 1636 and 1643, by a local stonemason, and there was never a nunnery established in the area, although the tradition persisted until recent times.

APPENDIX 6

'THE FORGOTTEN BURIAL PLACE'

In 1868, John Askham of Wellingborough wrote an evocative description of a visit to a long-disused burial place 'of the oldest body of Dissenters' in Wellingborough. Part is reproduced here. (The incident in the final paragraph, with its sinister connotations, would have been an ominous sight to those living in earlier, more superstitious times.)

Situated in an unfrequented part of the town away from any habitation, and totally unknown to hundreds of the inhabitants of Wellingborough, its only approaches long, sullen-looking, sombre lanes, which, even by day, have a cut-throat look about them, and by night present the 'beau ideal' of a ghost walk, is the disused, forgotten burial ground. Unwholesome, blear-eyed, rotting walls of eight or ten feet high on either side bound the dark lane leading to it, and in the crumbling carcase of one of these is a low-browed doorway, the door of which would be the entrance to the place of sepulture. Within, an oblong slip of earth, bounded on either side by allotment grounds, and divided from them by low, frowsy walls, near relations to the outer ones, forms the burial place.

The last occasion on which we visited the place was in the summer time; the old rickety door had been left unfastened, and was swinging to and fro on its rusty hinges, with a melancholy sound, as we entered. A wretched looking pony was blundering among the unkempt graves, and lifted up its head as if in mute protest at such sorry fare and ghostly quarters. Hassocks of rank, coarse grass had blotted out all traces of a path if there had ever been any. One of the tombs is fenced in by tottering palisades, near which a tree had been planted, but it had sickened and died, and its skeleton rattled ominously in the low summer wind. Other mementos and tablets stand or lie about in all directions. The flat ones seemed to be the favourite promenade of snails, for their surfaces were covered with slimy hieroglyphics left by their trail. Others lie about or stand at angles while some again are panelled into the rotting walls, down which green stains run down from the humid stones, and all have that peculiar mildewed appearance which gathers about such places seldom visited.

As we put aside the nettles with our foot to read the inscription on one of these, a large unwholesome black toad sprang out, and after eyeing us suspiciously, crawled underneath the wall. Of flowers, those beautiful offerings of affection at the shrines of the departed, there were none; the dead there seem to have died out of memory, and the shapeless graves, scattered about in higgledy piggledy disorder, looked deplorable …

BIBLIOGRAPHY

BOOKS AND ARTICLES (GENERAL INTEREST)

Anderson, M. D., *The Imagery of British Churches* (London: 1955).

Askham, John, *Sketches in Prose and Verse* (NMC, 1893).

Aston, Trevor, *Crisis in Europe 1560–1660* (London: 1965).

Barnum, P. H., ed., *Dives and Pauper* (Early English Text Society, 1976–80).

Boddington, A., *Raunds Furnell: The Anglo-Saxon Church and Churchyard* (English Heritage, 1996).

Buckberry, Jo, and Annia Cherryson, *Burial in Later Anglo-Saxon England* c. 650–1100 (Oxbow, 2010).

Burgess, Frederick, *English Churchyard Memorials* (Lutterworth Press, 1963).

Burn, J. S., *The History of Parish Registers in England* (2nd edn, 1862).

Bushnell, G. H., *The Monumental Brasses of Northamptonshire* (NAAS, 1850).

Caiger-Smith, A., *English Medieval Mural Paintings* (Oxford: 1963).

Chapman, Leigh, *Church Memorial Brasses and Brass Rubbings* (Shire, 1987).

Child, Mark, *Discovering Churchyards* (Shire, 1982).

Clarke, J. M., *The Dance of Death in the Middle Ages and Renaissance* (Glasgow: 1950).

Coleman, Thomas, *Memorials of the Independent Churches in Northamptonshire* (Snow, 1853).

Colvin, H., *A Biographical Dictionary of British Architects 1600–1840* (Yale University Press, 1997).

Cox, J. C., ed., *Churchwardens' Accounts, 14th to 17th Century* (1913).

Cox, J. C., ed., *The English Parish Church* (1914).

Cox, J. C., ed., *Parish Registers of England* (reprinted, EP, 1974).

Creighton, C., *A History of Epidemics in Britain* (F. Cass, 1965).

Daniell, C., *Death and Burial in Medieval England* (Routledge, 1997).

Deacon, Malcolm, *Philip Doddderidge of Northampton* (Northamptonshire Libraries, 1980).

Duffy, Eamonn, *The Stripping of the Altars* (Yale University Press, 1992).

Erbe, T., ed., *Mirk's Festival: A Collection of Homilies by Johannes Mirkus* (EETS, 1905).

Esdaile, Katharine, *English Monumental Sculpture since the Renaissance* (SPCK, 1927).

Esdaile, Katharine, *English Church Memorials* (Batsford, 1946).

Fell, Jenny, *Three Ells in Hellidon* (self-published, 2000).

Gittings, Clare, *Brasses and Brass Rubbings* (Blandford, 1970).

Gittings, Clare, *Death, Burial and the Individual in Early Modern England* (London: 1988).

Glass, Norman, *The Early History of the Independent Church at Rothwell* (Taylor, 1871).

Greenhill, F. A., *Incised Effigial Slabs c. 1100–c. 1700* (Faber, 1976).

Greenwood, D., *Who's Buried Where in England* (Constable, 1990).

Gunnis, R. F., *Dictionary of British Sculptors 1660–1851* (Odhams, 1953).

Happe, Peter, ed., *English Mystery Plays* (Harmondsworth, 1975).

Happe, Peter, ed., *Four Morality Plays* (Harmondsworth, 1987).

Hartshorne, A., *The Recumbent Effigies of Northamptonshire* (B. M. Pickering, 1876).

Hartshorne, C. H., *Historical Memorials of Northamptonshire* (Abel, 1848).

Hawthorn, Joseph, *Poems* (Kettering: Goss, 1882).

Hill, Peter, *Portrait of Great Oakley* (Orman, 1994).

Hill, Peter, *Rockingham Forest Revisited* (Orman, 1998).

Hill, Peter, *In Search of the Green Man in Northamptonshire* (Orman, 1996; rep. 1999).

Hill, Peter, *In Search of the Green Man* (Capall Bann, 2005).

Hill, Peter, *Folklore of Northamptonshire* (Tempus, 2005; rep. History Press, 2009).

Hill, Peter, *Secret Northamptonshire* (Amberley, 2009).

Hirst, L. F., *The Conquest of Plague* (OUP, 1953).

Hoskins, W. G., *Local History in England* (Longman, 1972).

Hudson, Franklin, *The Brasses of Northamptonshire* (McLean, 1853).

Hyett, W., *Sepulchral Monuments in the County of Northampton* (Nicolls, 1829).

Irons, A. E., *An Episcopal Visitation in 1570* (ns. 2, NNQ, 1907–09).

Jones, Graham, *Saints in the Landscape* (Tempus, 2007).

Jones, Jeremy, *How To Record Gravestones* (CBA/Rescue, 1976).

Keisler, D., *Stories in the Stone* (Smith, 2008).

Kemp, B., *English Church Monuments* (Batsford, 1981).

Klepper, E., *Costume through the Ages* (Dover, 2000).

Laslet, Peter, *The World We Have Lost* (Methuen, 1965).

Lewis, Shelagh, 'The Coxes of Northamptonshire' (*NPP* vol. 6, feature).

Lindley, K., *Of Graves and Epitaphs* (Hutchinson, 1965).

Longden, H. I., *The Visitation of the County of Northampton, 1681* (Harleian Society, 1935).

Lucy, S., and A. Reynolds, eds, *Burials in Medieval England and Wales* (Maney, 2002).

MacCracken, H., ed., *The Minor Poems of John Lydgate: Part One* (EETS, 1911).

Macklin, Herbert W., *The Brasses of England* (Methuen, 1913).

Markham, Christopher, *Hatchments* (NOASS, 1910).

Markham, Christopher, *The Churchyards of Northamptonshire* (NOASS, 1929).

Meaney, A., *Gazetteer of Early Anglo-Saxon Burial Sites* (1964).

Meech, S., and H. Allen, eds, *The Book of Margery Kempe* (Early English Text Society, 1940).

Mytum, Harold, *Recording and Analysing Graveyards* (Council for British Archaeology, 2000).

North, Thomas, *The Church Bells of Northamptonshire* (Clarke, 1878).

Peacock, E., ed. *Monuments of Superstition* (London: 1866).

O'Connor, M. C., *The Art of Dying Well* (New York: 1942).

Peacock, John, *Costume 1066 to the Present* (Thames and Hudson, 2006).

Percival, Spencer, *Executions in Northampton 1277–1893* (Taylor, 1900).

Percy, Thomas, *Réliques of Ancient English Poetry* (1765; Moxon, 1844).

Scarisbrick, J. J., *The Reformation and the English People* (OUP, 1984).

Settle, Alison, *English Fashion* (Collins, 1948).

Summers, Peter, and John Titterton, *Hatchments in Britain: Northamptonshire* (Phillimore, 1975).

Sutherland, Diana, *Northamptonshire Stone* (Dovecote Press, 2003).

Tate, W., *The Parish Chest* (CUP, 1969).

Thomas, Keith, *Religion and the Decline of Magic* (Penguin University Books, 1973).

Thompson, V., *Dying and Death in Later Anglo-Saxon England* (Boydell, 2004).

Tristram, E. W., *English Medieval Wall Painting* (London, 1944).

Vallance, Aylmer, *Old Crosses and Lychgates* (Batsford, 1920).

Victoria County History of England: Northamptonshire: Volume 1 (1902).

Vincent, W. T., *In Search of Gravestones, Old and Curious* (Mitchell & Hughes, 1896).

Whittick, A., *A History of Cemetery Sculpture* (London: 1936)   .

ARCHAEOLOGICAL BOOKS AND BOOKLETS

Archaeological Sites in Northamptonshire (4 vols, North West, North East, South West and Central, Royal Commission on Historical Monuments, 1975–82).

Chapman, A., D. Windell and J. Woodiwiss, eds, *From Barrows to Bypass: Excavation at West Cotton, Raunds* (Northamptonshire Archaeological Unit/English Heritage, 1990).

Harding, Jan, *Neolithic and Bronze Age Landscape in Northamptonshire: Raunds Area* (English Heritage, 2008).

Myres, J. N. L., *A Corpus of Anglo-Saxon Pottery* (2 vols, CUP, 1977).

Northamptonshire: An Archaeological Atlas (RCHM, 1980).

Pearson, Mike Parker, *English Heritage Book of Bronze Age Britain* (Batsford, 1993).

Pearson, Mike Parker, *The Archaeology of Death and Burial* (Sutton, 1999).

Taylor, Alison, *Burial Practices in Early England* (Tempus, 2001).

Tingle, Martin, ed., *The Archaeology of Northamptonshire* (Northamptonshire Archaeological Society, 2004).

Wild, Peter, ed., *Durobrivae, A Review of Nene Valley Archaeology: 9* (1984).

ARCHAEOLOGICAL REPORTS

Baker, R. S., 'On the Discovery of Anglo-Saxon Remains at Desborough, Northamptonshire' (*Archaeologia* 45, pp. 466–71).

Cox, J. C., ed., 'Chantry Certificates of Northamptonshire' (*Assoc. Architectural & Archaeological Reports* XXXI, 1911).

Cox, J. C., ed., 'The Parish Churches of Northamptonshire, Temp. Henry VIII' (*Archaeological Journal* XXX, 1913).

Cox, J. C., ed., 'The Parish Churches and Religious Houses of Northamptonshire: Their Dedications, Altars, Images and Lights' (*Archaeological Journal* LXXX, 1913).

Gibson, A. M., and A. McCormick, 'Excavations at Grendon Quarry, Northamptonshire: Part One' (*Northamptonshire Archaeology* 20, pp. 23–66).

Jackson, Dennis, 'The Excavation of Neolithic and Bronze Age Sites at Aldwincle, Northamptonshire 1959–1961' (*Northamptonshire Archaeology* 11, pp. 12–70).

Jackson, Dennis, 'Archaeology at an Ironstone Quarry in the Harringworth–Wakerley Area, 1968–1979' (*Northamptonshire Archaeology* 16, pp. 14–33).

Jackson, Dennis, 'The Excavation of a Bronze Age Barrow at Earls Barton' (*Northamptonshire Archaeology* 19, pp. 3–30).

Jackson, Dennis, 'Excavations at Wakerley, Northants, 1972–1975' (*Britannia* IX, pp. 115–288)

Meadows, Ian, 'Wollaston' (*South Midlands Archaeology* 25, pp. 41–5).

OTHER RECORDS

I have also consulted parish registers, wills and bequests, churchwardens' accounts, bishops' visitations, Quaker minute books, and the Rothwell Independent Chapel minute books.